DAD, AM I' GOING TO DIE?

DAD, AM I' GOING TO DIE?

LOVE, GRIEF, & BASKETBALL

DON CALVERT

Dad, Am I Going to Die?
Love, Grief and Basketball

If you look at the first stages of Joseph's life: it's full of tragedy and heartache and injustice and everything was a disaster. A book is meant to be read from beginning to end but this is best understood from the end to beginning. You'd think that he was a complete failure and that it was a shame that all those terrible things happened to him. However, you can't look at his life except in the context to the intended future God had for him and the ultimate completion of his life well lived and blessed beyond measure.

God was gracious enough to promise me a future before the tragedy and heart ache began. These promises helped me hold onto a life that seemed out of control and tragic for many years. But God had a plan and one that I'd like to share with you. Not so you'll feel sorry for me but so that you can meet the friend who walked with me as the suffering savior and as the healing balm of Gilead.

Some of you know Him through struggles and strife and have known the heartache and maybe these chapters can help with the healing and restoration. Some of you haven't experienced tragedies like this but maybe you can better know a savior who loves you desperately. Still others haven't begun this walk at all; let me begin to tell you what an incredible journey life can be when you are living it with Christ by your side.

The Calvert Family.
I'm the favorite son and brother.

CHAPTER 1
All About the Family

"Now faith is the evidence of things hoped for, the evidence of things not seen."

Hebrews 11:1

"Faith is not intelligent understanding, faith is deliberate commitment to a person where I see no way."

OSWALD CHAMBERS

(My favorite author) twentieth-century Stollish Baptist evangelist and teacher. He is best known for his devotional *"My Utmost for His Highest."*

My Dad was a basketball coach, so I was raised in a gym. My Dad played for the legendary basketball coach Mr. Henry Iba. I was born in Stillwater, Oklahoma in 1959. We moved a few times while I was growing up and the summer before my sophomore year in high school, we moved from Bridge City, Texas to Oklahoma City, Oklahoma where my dad was my coach for the next 3 years.

Starting at a new school again was probably the main reason I was so insecure in high school. Both of my parents were conservative Christians so if I wasn't in the gym, I was in church. My Dad always led the Fellowship of Christian

Athlete's group in every high school, so we attended about 8 or 9 FCA camps growing up. Each one was a great experience because I got to be around professional athletes like Donnie Perkins of the Dallas Cowboys, Emmit Thomas, Buck Buchanon, Willie Lanier of the Kansas City Chiefs, Bobby Richardson of the New York Yankees who talked about their relationship with Jesus Christ and challenged us to follow Christ and live our lives for Him. At every turn, I had great role models. By then, I already knew God had a plan for my life and that I could trust Him for my future.

"Another family picture but with my little sister Julie."

The Church I attended in high school was also attended by a young couple with the last name Shirley who's brother pitched for the Reds and Yankees. This couple led our Sunday School class where I had some close friends and enjoyed being a part of the group. Every summer, we'd attend an FCA camp, church camp and a mission trip somewhere together.

There was no doubt in my mind that I wanted to be a Christian at a young age and spend my whole life following God's unique plan for me. I knew God was alive and living in me. It wasn't that I deserved to go to Heaven or was a good person. With all my heart, I believed that Jesus died for me and rose from the grave and that by faith in His atonement for my sins, I was set free from the penalty of sin and now had a personal relationship with God my Father through His Son Jesus Christ. The greatest gift I've ever received is the gift of forgiveness and Christs atonement for my sin.

The second greatest gift was my parents. They raised my sisters and I to be in church. My Dad is a man of integrity that is trustworthy, always putting others first and practiced the golden rule. I've never heard my dad lie, curse or treat anyone without respect, even referees. We were taught to work hard and be disciplined. My sisters and I still talk about our chores on Saturdays. If we wanted to watch TV, it had to be done before 8am because the TV was off after that.

"THE GREATEST GIFT I'VE EVER RECEIVED IS THE GIFT OF FORGIVENESS AND CHRISTS ATONEMENT FOR MY SIN."

Our vacations were spent going to my grandparents' house or farm in Mountain View, Oklahoma, a farming community. It was expected that there was work to be done and we all pitched in. Of course, we had Church on Sundays, but also had fun, and did a whole lot of eating. As poor as we were, every holiday was spent with grandparents which was fine for my sisters and I because we loved it there.

Where my dad taught us integrity and character and to always do the right thing, my mom more than anyone, helped us understand the importance of having a personal relationship with Jesus Christ. Watching her read her Bible and kneel in prayer everyday helped prepare me for the years to come. I learned just how important having a quiet time with God everyday was and just how great was my need to depend upon Him. When I was bored my mom would tell me, "You don't need to be entertained all the time; sometimes you need to just sit and listen to God speak to you." She would consistently tell me that most things I wanted, I really didn't need. I didn't know it then but she was teaching me to be content. The most profound words ever spoken to me, were by my Mom in 1986 on a very dark day but that is for another chapter.

> **"AFTER WRITING A LIST OF 56 THINGS, I NEVER DOUBTED MY DAD'S LOVE AGAIN AND DIDN'T HAVE A SECOND THOUGHT ABOUT IT."**

Don't get me wrong, my parents weren't perfect. I still remember my dad grabbing me by the throat and slamming me against the wall one time when I made him mad at the gym. However, I don't remember what it was done for exactly. Dad never told me he loved me until I was in my fifties and that really bothered me growing up. When I was in high school and I was feeling sorry for myself, I was prompted by God, I believe, to write a list of all the ways my Dad showed me he loved me. After writing a list of fifty-six things, I never doubted my Dad's love again and didn't have a second thought about it. One of those ways was my Dad took me everywhere. He didn't take his friends, he took me and we had great times.

I remember going to OU football games together when they were ranked #1. They had Joe Washington, Steve Davis and the legendary Selmon brothers and it was a very exciting time. Dad had a friend that was a coach for the Oklahoma football team named Don Jimmerson and he would give us tickets occasionally.

Dad and I were there when Baylor upset OU in Norman, and when Kansas upset OU in 1975 when OU was ranked #2.

Baylor had a quarterback named Jeffries. He was known for overcoming his stutter, becoming a starter for Baylor, and upsetting one of the greatest teams in OU history on their home field. I got to hear the coach for Baylor that next summer talk at an FCA camp about that game; how his quarterback had gone the previous year from forgetting the number of downs left in a game and costing their team the win, to beating one of the great OU teams at home. I really loved inspirational stories like this growing up. I remember being at a game against Nebraska and we had a basketball game that night and needed to leave but the game was too exciting to leave. Dad and I waited at the top steps of the stadium and took off running as soon as OU had it in hand with a final interception. We ran about a mile to our car and barely made it to warm-ups for the game. It was worth all the effort and we, of course won or this would be a terrible story.

My favorite experience at the games was when Joe Washington, (who later played for the Washington Redskins) would go back to recieve the punt and the entire crowd would slowly rise to their feet because we knew that he was getting ready to do something special in his famous silver shoes. Dad and I were also at the game against Pittsburg when a freshman named Tony Dorsett was supposed to put on a show, but it was "Little Joe" that always brought the excitement. It was cool however to see Dorsett hurdle an OU defender on the sideline and not break stride. I bought into "OU magic" and would live and die on Saturdays with my Dad and Sooner football.

Dad would also take me over to Mr. Iba's house and we'd talk basketball for hours. I still have the Olympic pin and pictures he gave me from the "72 olympics. He talked about the upset against Russia and how he knew there was no chance the officials were going to let the USA win. Mr Iba is the person that got me started doing quickness and jumping drills, and would talk to me about shooting and how to get my shot-off quicker. When Mr. Iba died, it was a very sad day because he was my Dad's mentor. He would give Dad advice over the years on different jobs and positions. He would always call and give a recommendation for him.

> **"I STILL HAVE THE OLYMPIC PIN AND PICTURES HE GAVE ME FROM THE "72 OLYMPICS."**

When I was born in 1959 and dad had finished his 3rd year of playing basketball for Mr. Iba, he had to quit to go to work at a gas station to support our family. Mr. Iba came to the station and asked my dad what he really wanted to do in life and dad said "coach like you."

Mr. Iba made dad the freshman coach along with Eddie Sutton and that started his coaching career. Mom thought she was marrying a farmer.

Dad was close friends with Denny Price, whose 2 sons played in the NBA. He was the assistant coach for the Phoenix Suns at the time. We lived in Texas and when Phoenix would play in Houston, Dad and I would go spend the night with him, and sleep on the floor or couch in the hotel, and then go to the game.

Denny's two sons went on to play in the NBA and were both great players. Mark is known for starting the pick and roll with Brad Daugherty at Cleveland and was a great shooter who actually held the free throw percentage record for many years. When Pat Reilly was the head coach for the New York Knicks, a reporter asked him about all the dominating players in the NBA. He corrected the reporter and said there were only 3 dominating players in the NBA at the time, Michael Jordan of the Bulls, the Knicks Patrick Ewing, and Mark Price of the Cavaliers, according to Pat Reilly. One game his rookie year, Cleveland was playing at the Detroit Pistons. Mark got into a fight with Isaiah Thomas during the second half. Dad read in the paper about the fight the next day and called Denny to ask him when Mark had become a fighter.

Denny said he called Mark that night and asked him what happened. Mark told him that he had to fight because Thomas kept giving him little rabbit punches in the ribs as they were running side-by-side down the court. Mark needed to let Thomas and others know that although he was small for an NBA player, he wasn't going to be intimidated. It was against his Cleveland Cavaliers that Michael Jordan hit the famous "Shot on Ehlo" that ended the series and kept them out of the finals.

Another time when Denny Price was in Houston with the Phoenix Suns, we were eating lunch with him before the game and the players were all sitting around us. It's the first time I heard about players being paid off for college. He described to us how Keith Erickson, who was a guard for Phoenix at the time, had gotten paid at UCLA and how it all took place. Players were given a magazine when they arrived which basically had everything in it a young man would want, and they would pick out and basically order what they

wanted. There was a famous booster that would take care of everything. Denny told us beside the magazine transactions, Erickson wouldn't say much about who was getting what. A few years later, Denny did tell Dad and I how much Patrick Ewing got to stay at Georgetown his senior year and how much Wayman Tisdale got to stay at OU his junior year.

"*My Oklahoma University Letter Jacket.*"

My last year at OU, Mark was taking one of his five official visits to OU out of high school and my dad came over to Norman to visit Denny, Mark, and I. The thing I remember most about their visit was when I asked Denny if Mark was serious about signing with OU and he said, "Really no." Mark had learned that the assistant coach in charge of recruiting for Coach Tubbs didn't like white guards. Mark wanted to go where he was really wanted so he followed a new head coach to Georgia Tech and played along side great players like John Sally and Bruce Dalrymple.

Denny's youngest son Brent was also a great player and

ironically, after transferring from South Carolina, went on to play at OU and then on to play for 4 NBA teams from 1992-2002. Denny Price asked Dad to coach his sons in high school in Enid, Oklahoma but Dad was coaching at Barton County Community College at the time. Our family visited Enid and Dad thought about it long and hard but it wasn't the right move.

God had another plan for my Dad, which included me. Many years later, Denny Price would send me a letter saying I was one of the best instructors he had ever seen which gave me a lot of confidence.

He would call me on weekends and we'd talk for a couple hours about my "Score Basketball Program" and he'd ask a ton of questions about how and why I did certain things.

Interesting side story from the 1970's: Not many people know my dad was asked by John McCloud, coach at OU in the early '70's, to be his assistant coach along with Denny Price. Shortly after that was when they both went to the Phoenix Suns as the

"LIFE WOULD HAVE BEEN A LOT DIFFERENT IF DAD TOOK THE JOB AT OU AND WE FOLLOWED COACH MCCLOUD AND DENNY PRICE TO PHOENIX."

head and assistant coach. The only problem was Dad had just taken the head basketball job at Bartlesville Sooner High School and sometimes integrity gets in the way. As I understand it, dad felt it wasn't right or best to skip out now. Life would have been a lot different if dad took the job at OU and we followed Coach McCloud and Denny Price to Phoenix. I never regretted any of this because I knew God had a different and better plan for our lives, and I trusted that plan. I'll always remember the Final Four's, coaching clinics, basketball games and football games. If dad was going somewhere, I was going also.

Mom on the other hand was tough. She slapped the fire out of me a few times, which I enjoy reminding her of occasionally. Picking cotton and playing the piano made her very strong. She would grab me by that muscle between my shoulder and neck above my collarbone and squeeze it until I was brought to my knees.

I remember mom loving me, but like God's nature, there was the loving side, and then you were expected to do the "right thing"side. One of the most important things I learned from mom was to forgive and always give grace. I always wanted to do the right thing because I didn't want to disappoint my mom and dad. We had a strict house, but it wasn't a list of rules. It was about a relationship with Jesus Christ and wanting to glorify Him. My parents taught Christ through example mostly which has a profound affect.

Being raised with 3 sisters (a forth came along a few years later) who all loved the Lord Jesus and followed God made it easy for us to get along and enjoy each others company. Each one of my sisters have had their own struggles and trials but remain faithful to God. They would agree with me that we are very fortunate to be raised in the "Calvert Family" with the Christian heritage our grandparents, uncles, aunts and parents instilled and trained us in. The "Calvert Family Values" are our cornerstone and have given us great guidance throughout our lives. We had stability and strong faith that in just a couple years would prove critical to our lives that would be tested at every turn.

My Sophomore Year at OU.
Those are the pants that I kept slipping and falling in.

CHAPTER 2
Basketball Bliss

"And after the earthquake a fire;
but the Lord was not in the fire: and
after the fire a still small voice."

1 Kings 19:12

*If we let the Spirit of God bring us face to face with God, we shall
hear the still small voice of God; and in perfect freedom will say,
"Here I am, send me."*

OSWALD CHAMBERS

(Baptist preacher and evangelist)

After my senior year in high school, I was headed to OSU to play for Jim Killingsworth. However, God had other plans. Coach Killingsworth decided to leave OSU to take a coaching job at TCU. So I changed my mind and went to play for a new, young head coach at OU, named Dave Bliss.

Some very important things happened to me and for me during my first year at OU. Most of it was really hard but rewarding. Already, I was learning to be independent and rely upon God. My parents didn't drop me off at college; instead, they just said "Good luck." I only lived an hour away the first two years of college, so that made it easier.

I was an average basketball player on a very good young team. Four of the players would be drafted in the NBA in a couple years. Our daily practice averaged three hours a day. After the first couple of practices, I remember thinking "I have to do this everyday for the next four years and then go back to my room to study for 2-4 hours. "What did I get myself into?"

> ## "TO SAY PRACTICE WAS HARD WOULD BE AN UNDERSTATEMENT."

To say practice was hard would be an understatement; It was a mental and physical grind every time. Super-intense-Coach-Bliss was Bobby Knight's assistant at Indiana the year they went undefeated. He got the job at OU the next year. His tough, demanding, hard core attitude was the same as Coach Knight's. Coach Bliss could punt a basketball in Lloyd Noble Center as high and beautiful as Von Schamann did against Ohio State that year. Our trainer Pugs, would count how many rows "the kick" went up to see if it was a new record and report back to us in the locker room.

One time over Christmas holiday practices, two-a-days they were called, coach put us on the line for 30 minutes of line drills. Ironically, because I scored twice in a row on the scout team going 4-on-4. I got to play Darnell Valentine that week which meant I got to drive or shoot every time. Coach was so mad saying "With all due respect, if we can't stop DC, how can we stop Darnell Valentine?" Darnell went on to play for the Portland Trailblazers who by the way are now coached by two of my former teammates; Terry Stotts and John McCollough.

The Oklahoma University football team was ranked #1 in the country, and because of suspensions, only had to beat an undermanned Arkansas team to win the national championship.

Coach had the idea that a winning championship team should be willing to sacrifice and do what other teams are not willing to do, so we practiced during the game. As it turned out, we didn't miss much, but you get the idea. I still remember the next night, getting out of practice late and heading to the chow hall around 6:30 pm. The football team had just arrived at home and a couple of players joined Aaron, Al and myself. Darrel Ray was the starting safety who would later play for the National Football Leagues, New York Jets. He was frustrated and actually mad because a few players had stayed out all night and then didn't play well.

Guess that was the kind of sacrifice coach wanted us to devote ourselves to. Darrell said that he had heard some guys were out but when he woke up the next morning, he saw a group of about 6-8 players who were just coming in the hotel and had been out at bars all night, including one of the starting running backs, an offensive lineman, and a couple of defensive lineman, and some others. OU during the game, played uninspiring football and looked out of it most of the game and it made sense when we heard how many guys had stayed out all night.

I didn't get to suit up, or play at all during my first year at OU. Only practicing was emotionally demanding and very discouraging.

I played a lot of defense that first year. Coach brought me into his office before the games started and talked to me about his decision.

I totally got it because I wasn't very good then. There were three or four other guys that weren't very good on the team either. Not only did I not suit up, I wasn't even practicing much.

The hardest part was that the coaches basically ignored me. It's difficult thinking you don't belong or aren't wanted. Of course, I thought about quitting many times but there was no way I would ever follow through because I knew God had a plan and I didn't want to miss out on it. Plus, I was tough-minded and stubborn. The training was beginning and it was training I needed. I didn't know it at the time but this was the start of an important journey that had a destination and purpose.

That night, I called my parents about the meeting. Dad called me back later with some scripture verses to encourage me. They knew I was very down. This started a lifelong habit that became very important. When life gets hard; discouraging or confusing, the Word of God becomes my anchor.

That year '77-78, I spent a ton of time in the Bible. Another key thing happened that year was when God blessed me with a mentor who took me under his wing. I started attending the Baptist Student Union where there was a man named Max Barnett, who encouraged me each week. He instilled in me the importance of trusting God everyday and spending time in the Word of God, just as my mom had done for years. Everyday I knew that God wanted to talk to me, lead me, encourage me and especially love me. His emphasis was the importance of memorizing scripture and "hiding it in my heart." The Fellowship of Christian Athletes meetings I tried once were shallow. I really wanted to grow and needed to get serious about who God was to me.

It was the loneliest I had ever been, but in the quiet times of the day, God spent time revealing Himself to me and growing my relationship with Him.

My freshman year, I gave my best effort in practice everyday and worked hard at my grades. Slowly, I started to improve on the court. My main goal was to reflect Christ Jesus everyday and survive practice.

> **"WHEN LIFE GETS HARD; DISCOURAGING OR CONFUSING, THE WORD OF GOD BECOMES MY ANCHOR."**

I would pray before practice in my dorm room expecting and trusting that God would be with me. I had to go to study hall for the first month but when Coach Ash saw my grades, he said I didn't need to waste my time.

It was interesting though, there were two young ladies who would tutor us when we needed it. I hated for her to come to my desk because she was the first girl I had been around who didn't shave her underarms. Worst thing was, she also liked wearing sleeveless blouses. I liked her well enough, it was just gross having her lean over me with those hairy armpits.

I did get a tutor provided by the athletic department one year when I needed help in a writing class.

Ironically after all these years, I still remember some of the things she taught me.

I now know that God was leading me to be internally motivated, not externally. When you are motivated internally, the daily struggles of life can't get to you because your hope is in Christ, your self-worth is in Christ, your ability to be consistent in effort and focus is in Christ which strengthens you. I can then die to myself and live for Christ.

Perceived rejection and criticism doesn't affect you as much because I wasn't playing basketball for a coach, my parents, or for recognition; but for Christ.

If I was going to be strong-minded and handle what life threw at me, then I needed to learn who I was in Christ, and live from that internal prompting and conviction, not from the world's perspective and exterior motivation. Talk about a hard but important lesson. The Bible says in 2 Timothy 1:7:

For God has not given us a spirit of fear but of love, power and a strong mind.

I was going to need all three to survive and God was working on me daily. Loving people I didn't really like became a choice everyday, not something I'd do because I felt like it. Satan comes to steal, kill and destroy. So I needed to learn to control my mind and my emotions; It took the Word of God for me to retrain my mind, so that Satan couldn't discourage me, beat me down or make me negative. A strong mind controlling my thoughts, relying on the power of God and not my feeble attempts at doing good was something I had to grow mature in and make a habit of.

An interesting thing started to happen; God began to reveal himself to me and his plans for my future. In Ephesians 2:10, God tells us "For we are God's workmanship, created in Christ Jesus to do good works, which God prepared in advance for us to do." God knew the path I was on, I needed to know that He was definitely with me and in charge. My mom told me that God had never led her in this way and I didn't know anyone else who God had laid out their future like this for them.

Questioning each "word" I'd get from God, the future was being laid out for me. I didn't ask for it and really didn't have anything like this happen before but I knew God was talking to me.

The first thing God shared with me was that I'd meet my wife on Pentecost day. I had no idea what that meant. Remember, I had no experience with this sort of thing. Next, God informed me that I would have two boys. Third, that I would influence many people. Forth, God would use me to help with families. Fifth, no disease would overtake me. All of these promises would further cement my commitment and faith in God's plan. Two of these promises wouldn't take place for many years and still haven't been fully fulfilled; yet.

The next 14 years would be a time of growing and waiting on God. There was no way for me to understand the "weight" of these promises or how critical the tests and learning would be. I thought I was ready for whatever life threw at me. I was wrong.

John McCollough, Aaron Curry, & Al Beal carrying me off the court after hitting my first shot at OU. I'm sure it would have been "3" if there was 3's back then.

CHAPTER 3
Being Carried Off the Court

"And God hath chosen the foolish
things of the world to shame the
wise; God chose the weak things of
the world to shame the strong."

1 Corinthians 1:27

*"In the history of God's work you will nearly always find that it
has started from the obscure, the unknown, the ignored, but the
steadfastly true to Jesus Christ."*
- OSWALD CHAMBERS
(Baptist preacher and evangelist).

"And without faith it is impossible to please God, because anyone who comes to him must believe that he exists and that he rewards those who earnestly seek him." Boy, can God change things quickly. I Really wasn't expecting much out of my sophomore year, and wasn't looking forward to much of anything, but God was continually building my faith and dealing with my insecurities. Becoming "strong in the Lord" and relying on His plan for my life was emphasized wherever I turned.

An interesting thing happened also. All the guys I didn't care for much were gone, transferred out.

"I'm the short one in the picture."

Not only that but when practice started, I was on the floor all the time. Practice was still tough but at least I had a meaningful role as a practice player. Our team started out the year slow. We won a tournament in Florida but didn't play well at San Francisco or Pepperdine. Back in 1979, there was a preseason Big 8 tournament. We lost to Kansas and played poorly and then took on Nebraska in a consolation game and looked even worse. Coach was so upset. I happened to be outside the bus and overheard him talk to Coach Ashe about not letting us go home for Christmas. Fortunately, he changed his mind.

When we got back a few days later, we had two-a-days before we opened up in a week with Kansas for the Big 8 opener. They had gone to the Final Four the year before and were loaded. Kansas was coached by Ted Owens who would run these baseline picks with their two seven foot guys, Moekeski and Von Moore. This was the week I got to play Darnell Valentine. We had great practices and went on to upset Kansas in the season opener for the Big 8. Earlier in the year, we had lost at Arkansas by five with the great Sydney Moncrief, so I knew we had a chance to be pretty good. I remember after the game, sitting in the back of the old locker room at Barnhill Arena with John McCollough, where we had to lean forward to get dressed because the locker room in the back slanted clear to the floor and of course the short guy needed to sit in the back.

Pugs, our manager, brought us the stats after the game on the stats sheet. John took a look at the stats and Moncrief had 32 points. He looked at me and said "I sure shut him down, didn't I?"

It was the start, of a historic season at the time. Lloyd Noble Center was packed every Big 8 game and was a lot of fun. We won the Big 8 for the first time in over 30 years and won at places like Kansas State that we hadn't won at in about the same time. Coach had us run a match up zone during each Big 8 game that gave teams fits. No one had seen it in our league and every game we'd make a "run" using it.

"ON THE ROAD WAS ALWAYS INTERESTING."

I played in about ten games that year but only in mop up duty when we were ahead quite a bit. It was fun hitting my first shot and having Aaron, Al, and John carry me off the court. I have a picture of the occasion in my office which brings back good memories. My favorite week of practice was when our starting point guard was hurt and couldn't practice the entire week. Coach had me run the first team all week and things went well. It was the week of our last (and clinching) game against Coach Hartman and the Kansas State Wildcats, for the Big 8 Championship.

It was always interesting on the road. At Nebraska, the student section would arrive really early to harass the opposing team. This game, I happened to be the one. The students serenaded me with "coaches son" and "Opey." Players were asking me what I did to get this response.

The most exciting game was at Kansas. We were down most of the game but were coming back, only down by five.

With a couple minutes left, Darnell Valentine stole the ball and was going in for a breakaway dunk, but Terry Stotts decided to deck him. It only happened because Terry couldn't jump.

Needless to say, there was pandemonium on the court. Coach Ted Owens ran over to our bench and grabbed Coach Bliss and yelled something you couldn't hear at him. Both benches emptied, but nothing happened besides both of us yelling. Having 15,000 crazy fans coming out of the stands was no fun, but it was exciting.

One of our trips was to the west coast to play Pepperdine and San Francisco. The part I remember the most was first of all, taking my first plane trip, but also driving up to the hotel in our van in San Francisco and seeing a guy eating food out of the trash can and then looking over to see two guys holding hands and kissing. Guess I wasn't in Oklahoma any more.

We played on the old San Francisco Dons basketball court. Towards the end of the game, my roommate Kyle Dodd, whispered to me that if he didn't go find a bathroom right then, there was going to be an unfortunate accident on the court and not the kind you're used to. I laughed so hard that I'm sure it didn't help matters. Disaster was averted and Kyle wasn't called upon during his absence, so coach didn't even know he was gone for awhile.

I loved Alcatraz, the many bridges, and all of the sight seeing. A couple of days later, we were in Los Angeles to play Pepperdine. Jerry West and Reggie Jackson walked in with us to the arena, which was pretty cool.

It was surprising to me how short Jackson was and how tall Jerry West was. Reggie Jackson made me feel tall which was hard to do. We didn't play very well in Pepperdines' high school atmosphere gym.

Later in the year, we were playing Kansas State in an important home game and we were warming up. The two referees called me over to half court. They informed me that they enjoyed calling our games because I was short like them and they didn't have to look up to me. Really, I wasn't that short but on the basketball floor, 5"11' is pretty much considered vertically challenged. Of course, I told them thanks, I think?

Aaron Curry once told me in the locker room that if my bolled legs would straighten out, I'd be as tall as everyone else. Terry Stotts did tell me once that I was fortunate to not be tall because I could walk into any store and buy clothes that would fit. Back then, there were no big and tall stores and there was not much available.

The first game I suited out was a home game. The warm up pants were so long that I kept tripping in warmups. Before the next game, my mom drove down to the game and sewed the pants up before the warmups started while sitting in her car. That was big time D1 basketball. Funny the things you remember 40 years later.

The last regular season game of the year was at home against Kansas State. The game was a sell out. If we won, we held sole possession of first place in the Big 8 for the first time in 30 years. Needless to say, things were very intense in the locker room.

Coach Bliss had just started to give us his pre-game speech, which was always really good, when suddenly there was a knock on the locker room door.

Coach was very annoyed, you could tell. The college president, Mr. Banowski introduced himself and went on to wish us good luck. Coach Bliss in his normal fashion, told him we needed to concentrate instead. Banowski apologized for the interruption and quickly left. The exchange was uncomfortable but Coach Bliss didn't care about that. Remember, Bobby Knight was his mentor.

The real excitement was about to begin. We cut down the nets after beating Kansas State at home and got ready for the Big 8 post season tournament the next week.

The part I remember most was my father getting to attend the games in Kansas City. Our family was always broke and couldn't afford much, but God provided. There was a man that came to many of our practices. Coach Bliss didn't let just anyone watch. He was the "O" Club President for the basketball team and was always really nice to me. He was talking to my father after one of our games and asked him if he knew why he came to our practices. My dad of course said no. Maybe exaggerating a little, he said that I was his favorite player to watch in practice because I was the best passer that he had ever seen at OU. He got to know my father and asked him if he was going to Kansas City for the Big 8 tournament. Dad had to decline because of money. The guy paid for my dad's bus ticket and let him stay in his hotel room. I was able to take care of his tickets and shared my meal money with him. It turned out to be a great week.

We were playing really well and ran through the postseason Big 8 tournament, beating Kansas again in the finals.

The NCAA tournament week was a blur. We received a bye for the first round and played Texas in the second round that Saturday in Dallas at the SMU gymnasium. The game was exciting and close throughout, but we pulled away

"OUR FAMILY WAS ALWAYS BROKE AND COULDN'T AFFORD MUCH BUT GOD PROVIDED."

and won by 10. The next game was against undefeated Indiana State with the great Larry Bird for the Sweet 16 in Cincinnati Ohio in front of 17,000 screaming fans. The game was really hyped up and was the game of the week shown nationally. There was no way OU was going to be allowed to win. The NCAA needed Larry Bird to play nationally in front of millions of fans.

The first half was really tough. The only problem was that we were in terrible foul trouble at halftime. It was pretty dire circumstances. We hadn't been in foul trouble the entire year. ISU went on to win and pulled away at the end. Coach surprisingly put me in with about 1 minute to go which made my heart skip a beat. Honestly, even though we lost, it was exciting to get to play and even got a shot up.

Coach Bliss barely said anything after the game. No praise or congratulations or pride in accomplishment, just disappointment. Flying home the next day, he kept to himself the entire trip. We had a long layover in Indianapolis and no words were exchanged. I was watching carefully and thought how sad that guys felt like they had failed. OU just had the best year in about 30 years but only the "agony of defeat" was experienced.

The thing I remember the most was getting to eat next to Larry Bird in the hotel restaurant later that night. He was very gracious and visited with me for quite awhile.

"GOD WAS PREPARING ME FOR A LIFE THAT WOULD BE USED FOR HIS PURPOSES AND GLORY."

Of course, I got an autograph which is in my office with other OU memorabilia. My dad and I were excited when he got drafted by our favorite team, the Boston Celtics.

My junior year started with high expectations. We graduated only two players that year but one of them was John McCollough, who was the player of the year in the Big 8 and who later got drafted by the Phoenix Suns.

We had picked up a couple of good players but didn't have the same chemistry. Bo Overton was a cocky freshman that wasn't respecting our point guard. I could see it coming. After practice one day, Raymond came in the locker room and quietly and unabashedly punched Bo in the face. Bo didn't look up or say anything. He knew Raymond would "clean his clock" if he came back at him. I could see his eyes watering like crazy. Nothing was said by anyone and we had good leadership because respect was instantly earned and nothing more needed to be done the rest of the year.

Saturday morning practices were brutal. They would last from 9am to 12pm most Saturdays and I would play a ton of defense. One of my favorite players on the team, not because I liked him a whole lot, but because he was so goofy and entertaining, was Ingram Purvis. Guys thought for sure with

that name, he was black, but he was whiter than me (which is saying a lot.) He did have a big white curly afro though. One game we were warming up and Purvis was complaining about his new shoes hurting his feet.

"Tournament in my junior year. Short shorts and why is Al so unhappy?"

When we got to the locker room for the pre-game speech, he took his shoes off and noticed that he had forgotten to take the paper wad out of the end of his shoes. When he'd make a mistake in practice, he'd immediately do push-ups sometimes as a self-imposed punishment. That was Ingram Purvis. Coaches always put me with him on road trips to room together. Probably because I could get along with everyone. Every trip he would talk about quitting and I'd work to talk him out of it. He did transfer after the season. I used to tell him that he was just homesick and it would get better. He was from Florida which was a long ways away.

The only good part about Saturday practices was looking forward to our football team crushing someone later that day. One early Saturday morning, Coach was talking, and one of the players started one of those really long morning yawns. Coach I guess felt disrespected and hit him in the face with a basketball and kept on talking. Needless to say, we had a lot of yawns that would be "eaten" after that.

It was hard not to smile when you'd see someone catch themselves while starting to yawn.

For the most part, all my years at OU, our teams got along well, but especially our championship season. Coach used to say that more teams break-up off the court with stuff, than ever do on the court.

He once told us over Christmas our championship year, when we were struggling, that he could make a call right then and could get every one of us a new car but that wouldn't be right and we weren't Kansas. We weren't going to cheat.

When he left the locker room, four or five guys fell to the floor in disbelief . They were imagining what car they could have. The joke on the team was you could tell the difference between the football and basketball teams parking lot. I still remember Al Beals beat up old station wagon he drove. How he got a girlfriend (and eventually his wife) driving that old thing, I'll never know.

Some wonderful things happened my first 3 years at OU. These things were meant to prepare me for the trials that would begin shortly.

First, my relationship with God grew tremendously. God had spent many a lonely night speaking to me and revealing himself to me, and I was learning to trust God and wait on Him.

Secondly, I learned that God is a rewarder of those who will believe Him and remain faithful. He started teaching me to live according to His promises.

Lastly, I learned that God was preparing me for a life that would be used for His purposes and glory. I didn't know any other way. God had humbled me and then exalted me in a short period of time. At that point, I was excited to see what God was going to do next.

This is how I like remembering the "boys."

CHAPTER 4

Quick Marriage and Coaching Girls

"And blessed is he, whosoever shall not be offended in me."

Matthew 11:6

"The danger with us is that we want to water down the things that Jesus says and make them mean something in accordance with common sense; if it were only common sense, it was not worthwhile for Him to say it."

- OSWALD CHAMBERS

(Baptist Preacher and noted author)

I was finishing up finals my junior year and packing up to go to my parents for the summer in Kansas, when God stopped me dead in my tracks the day before I was to leave. My dad had taken a job at Barton County Community College which was part of God's plan for my life.

Remember God telling me he had a wife for me and that it would happen on Pentecost Day? Well, I didn't know it was an actual day. After finals were over that week, I was looking at my calendar and it had inscribed Pentecost Day on the calendar for that next Sunday. Immediately, God brought back to my mind from 2 years earlier, the promise he had made me. The whole day, I spent hours praying and reading the Bible. God led me to withdraw from college, which I did of course.

> **"IF YOU ARE FOLLOWING GOD'S LEAD BY FAITH, HE WILL ASK YOU TO DO THINGS THAT CAN'T BE EXPLAINED AND OTHERS WON'T UNDERSTAND."**

Ironically, Coach Bliss had resigned from OU anyway and had taken the head coaching position at Southern Methodist University.

My last final was on Wednesday, but I didn't go to Kansas until Friday morning because I wanted to make sure I was hearing from God correctly. Remember this faith walk thing was new to me. Of course, I didn't talk to my parents or any one else about what I was thinking. Oswald Chambers says that if you are following God's lead by faith, He will ask you to do things that can't be explained and others won't understand.

Pentecost Day, the holiday that is remembered by Christians as the day the Holy Spirit came to earth to live inside of Christians, as I mentioned, was that Sunday. I joined my parents for church that day, having no idea what was to happen. While sitting in Sunday School, a young lady walked in the class. Later after church, we started talking and she invited me over to her house later that afternoon. That started a whirlwind relationship. We were engaged that summer and married shortly thereafter.

I knew God had her picked out for me and I was following His timing. Don't get me wrong, I knew this was terribly unusual. Like God always does, He provided me with the perfect government job for the summer so that I made good money, and he even worked it out for me to have the last 2 weeks off with pay, which was perfect for the wedding and short honeymoon. A number of my friends and relatives were able to attend the wedding. It was a great week of fun and games that my father put together. The wedding was simple, but the kind that the Calverts have; God honoring and inexpensive. The college where my father coached, hired me on their maintenance staff which worked out well because I could watch practice and attend the games. We rented a nice duplex and started out fine enough. My wife, Martha and I didn't know each other when we got married. I learned that she was raised in a broken home with an abusive stepfather and had run away from home when she was 13, and had been taken care of by foster parents ever since. She was going to school at Barton County Community College to be a nurse which would really pay off later on in God's plan.

My Dad had always been a boys basketball coach in high school but now had been trying to get a college job. My last two years in high school, we had good years, upsetting the number one team in the state both years. We lost a heart-breaker my senior year in the semifinals of the state tournament on a last second shot.

Dad applied for the boys job at Barton County College. They gave the job to another coach but the athletic director liked my Dad so much that dad was promised that if he took the girls job, when the boys job opened up, he would get the boys job, so he took it. As always though, God had a different plan.

Dad had recruited well and had a great team that made it to the Final Four of the National Junior College Championships. In a tough game, Barton County lost to the eventual National Champion.

It was an exciting and fun year basketball wise, but also very trying. Growing up my family had always been at peace and there really wasn't any strife in the home. Needless to say, I was ill equipped to handle a young wife who was struggling personally with life. It became apparent that she was hoping I could make her happy and content, but that was impossible. Honestly, I had no idea how to deal with Martha's hurt and the pain she felt. Having been abused, there was tremendous unrest, anger and unforgiveness that would take her years to be healed from. I loved her very much but I'm sure I made tons of mistakes in trying to be a Godly husband.

As always though, God had a plan. He was training me to further wait on Him and to be grounded in His Word. Becoming dependent upon Him was imperative. Things were confusing at times and hard because God put me in the position to have to trust Him as my source for everything.

At the end of the summer, I had already enrolled at Oklahoma University to finish my last year. We had rented married university housing and moved into a nice apartment in August.

First thing I did was to go meet with new head basketball coach Billy Tubbs and ask to be part of the basketball program as a student assistant. Coach Tubbs was a great motivator. He made things exciting and fun. Our first meeting with him at the end of my junior year in the TV room at the athletic dorm was quite memorable. The conversation went something like this: "You guys know how your team would dribble down the court slowly and pass the ball around 20 times until you get the perfect shot? Well, we aren't going to do that anymore. It's too boring and so now if you come across half court and you're open, you better put it up." When he closed the short meeting, Raymond, Chucky and others were noticeably excited by the new approach. Coach Tubbs was very gracious and allowed me to attend and help in practice. However, none of the coaches knew me at all. I blame myself and my insecurities for not taking more advantage of the situation. After a month of watching from the sidelines, I went to work at the local sporting goods store instead of staying the course and earned some money for our family instead.

The end of the school year, we had an exciting addition that for me, began life in the real world. Cary Matthew Calvert was born on July 11, 1982. I was very proud and excited to have such a beautiful young son. From day one, Cary gave me great joy and happiness. What I was about to learn though, was my greatest source of joy would also become my greatest source of pain. After graduation, Martha and I decided to move to Bethany, just outside of Oklahoma City where I lived in high school. We didn't have a job yet, even though I was applying for coaching jobs in the area.

We didn't want to move anywhere until Cary was born, so I didn't start applying for jobs till after July 11th, Cary's birthdate.

There weren't many jobs available by then and we wanted to stay in the area. I trusted God was leading me where to go and I was praying for guidance everyday. The night before going to Bethany to find a job and a house, Martha told me she wanted a house with a strawberry garden and pecan trees. I'm pretty sure she was halfway joking. The next morning, I left Martha and Cary in Norman to go look at five or six houses a realtor had found for us. He took me to a house that needed lots of work but had lots of potential. My parents, as they had been doing, helped us financially, so we could afford the house. Coincidentally, when we looked in the back yard, it had a strawberry patch and pecan trees. God works in mysterious ways.

That year was a time of waiting on God. I took a job roofing houses and spent most of my time working on our house. It needed everything from floors, to walls, ceilings, bathrooms, sidewalks and windows. My favorite time was playing with Cary. He had a smile that was incredibly contagious and would help me with everything and get into everything.

The work was really hard. I'd work all day and then come home and work on the house until bedtime. One afternoon that is indelibly imprinted on my mind, God spoke to me again about my future which would include helping families to grow strong and help to restore them. The conversation I had with God that day was a cornerstone of things to come.

In the meantime, my dad applied for the head women's basketball coach at Oral Roberts University in Tulsa, Oklahoma. The thought of working with my dad and in college was exciting. I kind of assumed, he would want me as his assistant. Never really thought about coaching girls but being raised with three sisters, I did have experience.

Sure enough, Dad got the job. Having to wait for a month before dad was "allowed" to hire me was no fun and I'm sure I was very impatient. The house was now in good shape and ready to be sold. Finally, ORU's athletic director approved the hire and we were off to Tulsa. The pay was terrible but we moved into a nice condo that was owned by an ORU alum, so we got a discount.

Our first year was very successful. I was on the road recruiting very hard because we needed to get players in to build on. We upset some teams and finished with a winning record.

"THE CONVERSATION I HAD WITH GOD THAT DAY WAS A CORNERSTONE OF THINGS TO COME."

By April, we were able to sign really good players, 2 of which are in the ORU Hall of Fame. Vivian Herron led the nation in scoring one year and Kim Ogden was a terrific leader that was a really tough point guard from North Dakota and talked funny. When I recruited Kim, it wasn't that she was a great player or athlete, but that her intangibles were off the charts. This was the kind of leader that every program needed. Vivian on the other hand, was all about potential. She only started one year in high school. She attended school

 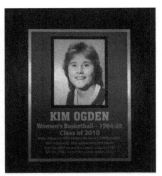

"Vivian & Kim's Hall of Fame pictures."

in Jackson Mississippi, and wasn't being recruited, but I could tell she was going to be a star. Her personality, cockiness, and fearlessness made a great impression on me right off. We always loved being around each other and she would inspire and encourage me by her tremendous attitude. Kim provided the toughness and leadership, Vivian gave us the confidence and aggressiveness.

The team had another assistant who wasn't really a basketball coach. Her father was a big donor to the school and that turned out to be a problem later on. She was also the women's athletic director, but my dad was promised by Larry Cochell, the Head Athletic Director that our program wouldn't be under her control.

However, our second year was rough. Sherry, our best player and our only married player got pregnant and had to red shirt. We were now starting all freshmen and sophomores and had only freshman and sophomores on the bench. Recruiting and developing players were our main goals. We were building for long term. The schedule was brutal and we only won a few games, but we weren't discouraged. Jerry Lucas of the famed New York Knicks had a daughter that was a freshman on our team at center, and we were starting talented players at every position. They were just too inexperienced. Recruiting was also going well so our third year held lots of promise. The next year would be our best, but it would also be the roughest.

I remember that summer, going over to Mr. Iba's house with him, asking every question you could think of. He was always so gracious and helpful, and would give me different memorabilia to take home.

I still have a copy of the cassette tape that I had put on a CD (that we recorded), to remember the great times we always had together.

Early years were so much fun.

CHAPTER 5

My Greatest Source of Joy was My Greatest Source of Pain

"My help cometh from the Lord, which made heaven and earth."

Psalm 121:2

It does not matter what evil or wrong may be in the way, He has said "I will never leave thee."

- OSWALD CHAMBERS

(Baptist Preacher and noted author)

The 60-story, City of Faith towers and hospital were built before we arrived and it was a blessing to our family and a curse. My family spent a lot of time there and the doctors and nurses were first class. The only problem was the hospital was a huge drain on the school. About that same time, all of the TV evangelist scandals were happening and the Oral Roberts Evangelistic Association donations were also way down. However, all of this was part of God's plan for our family.

Our second son, Aaron Keith, was born the first year we were in Tulsa. We started noticing that Cary wasn't growing normal and his development wasn't progressing the way he should have been. Cary wasn't very big, so everyone thought the boys were twins for awhile. Cary looked normal and people would comment how big his muscles were.

He was such a vibrant kid that loved to run and climb on anything, fearlessly. He was older than his Aunt Julie who would come over frequently, and he loved to wrestle with her and his brother and me.

He especially loved to swing as high as I could push him. I put up a swing set in the back yard and would push the boys on the swing everyday. He couldn't ride his bike very well so I kept training wheels on the bike for a long time. Best thing I ever got him was a red jeep that drove on a battery. It was great because we lived in a culdesac and the boys would spend hours riding the jeep. I did have to explain to Cary that no, you can't run over the neighborhood kids

"One of my favorite pictures."

in the jeep, even if they are rude to you. He couldn't retaliate physically, so he'd do it with his jeep.

His favorite thing to do was play baseball so I would pitch to him and try to hit the bat as much as possible. He couldn't swing the bat very good but would try really hard. He would wear his hat on backwards, hit the ball and take off running for first base.

That's when I indoctrinated him into loving the St. Louis Cardinals. Later on, I bought Cary a batting tee to make it easier for him and me.

We loved to go bike riding and one year we bought bike seats for the boys to ride on the back of our bikes. We would ride a couple of miles and then stop off at the park awhile to swing and climb and then head back to the house. Those were really good times and great memories.

More hours were spent on the floor than any other place, playing with Legos and Duplos.

The boys would get mad at me because I would take the best Legos so I could build really cool castles or cars or anything else we could think of.

"Boys stayed close for years."

We were excited about Aaron and Cary and really enjoying them both, but we kept wondering what was going on with Cary. It wasn't a huge concern at this point but decided to take him to the doctor to find out if there was anything medically we needed to know about.

Martha would have great days and we'd have a normal happy family and then there would be days where she would really struggle. Most of the time I really had no idea how to handle the different situations. She spent three or four different times at the City of Faith because she was hurting a tremendous amount and was crying out for help. Life was becoming more complicated but God, I knew, was still my source and strength and He was growing me up daily through struggles and hardships.

Not only was my wife in the hospital often that year, but so was Aaron. He was sick a lot and we almost lost him a couple of times with asthma before we got him to the emergency room. During a 6 month period, Cary, Aaron, and Martha were in the hospital 10 times. All this was really hard but was nothing compared to what was coming next.

"WITHOUT TRYING TO BE TOO DRAMATIC, THIS WAS THE START OF THE "DARK CLOUD" THAT WOULD ALWAYS ACCOMPANY ME AND STILL DOES TO THIS DAY."

The doctors wanted to run tests on Cary. We did a liver biopsy and muscle biopsy but didn't know why yet. I still remember Cary laughing at me because every time he'd get an IV, I'd start to faint and it became regular practice for the nurses to bring a bed in the room for me to lay on. Cary would tease me, asking if I didn't like blood. It was comic relief that would help him forget about the procedure.

He also had a bear with him always that became his constant companion which I still have in my office in a shadow box with his Mickey Mouse watch and his cross necklace.

Finally, after all the tests, the doctors set up a meeting at the old Children's Hospital offices with Martha and I. We walked in not having any idea what to expect.

The doctor went on to explain to us that Cary had Deuschennes Muscular Dystrophy and there was no cure and no treatments. I remember thinking that I just needed to talk to God. I needed to hear from Him and let Him tell me what the truth is. He had promised me two boys, and had promised me before I was even married, that no disease would ever overtake me. I also remembered that as we were walking back to the car, we were both in shock and didn't say a word driving home. Without trying to be too dramatic, this was the start of the "dark cloud" that would always accompany me and still does to this day. From now on, Cary and the "burden of disease," would be there. Ever since that day, depression would be a constant burden and battle.

Soon after, I called my mom because she always helped give me perspective and I wanted to hear from her what God would say to me, not just empty words.

She told me that my life would never be easy but that it would only get better because now I would have a relationship with God that most people would never have because I would have to depend on Him. She was right. Like I mentioned before, my greatest source of joy was now my greatest source of pain.

I learned a song that I would listen to often and sing within my darkest days. It went like this:

I walked a mile with pleasure,

she chatted all the way,

Leaving me none the wiser,

with all she had to say.

I've walked a mile with sorrow,

never a word said she.

From all the things I've learned from her,

Sorrow walked with me.

by Barry McGuire

Soon after this, God spoke to me dramatically in an unusual way. My car broke down and we didn't have cell phones back then. Fortunately, I made it to a garage and waited while they fixed my car because I couldn't get a hold of Martha or anyone else to pick me up. I sat there for hours waiting and read a lot of magazines. At the end of three hours, I read a short story from the Guidepost magazine about a family going through a tough time. I don't remember much about the story but God gave me a promise in that story that would carry me for years. The verse I read was Jeremiah 29:11 which says: "For I know the plans I have for you, declares the Lord, plans to prosper you and not to harm you, plans to give you hope and a future." The second I read the verse, Martha called the garage back to come and pick me up. I knew the message God wanted to make clear to me that day and I chose to lean on that truth from that day forward.

While all of this was going on, we started our third year at ORU. We were starting two sophomores, one freshman, one junior, and one senior. Sherry was back from having a child. We had a good young bench and we were building a really strong team. Recruiting was also going great.

We were in position to sign the best players ORU had ever had on campus for the women's program.

The #2 ranked team in college basketball, Louisiana Tech came to ORU. We got beat by 2 and had the ball with a chance to win at the buzzer. The schedule was tough again but we upset some quality teams and finished 18-10.

"Cary loved birthdays."

Larry Cochell was the athletic director at the time. Remember our other assistant coach and ORU's money problems brought on by the City of Faith Hospital and all the scandals? Larry told my dad that the Roberts were looking to make a change and give the other assistant the head coaching position, not for any good basketball reason.

What I was really concerned about was that we needed the insurance and the job stability with all the stress on our family. Things were hard enough without this mess going on.

After a week or so of hearing rumors, Larry called dad and I into his office and told us the news. Richard Roberts was firing dad and I, and making the other assistant the head coach because her father promised that he would underwrite the business school for $1 million if they would hire his daughter as the head coach.

> **"GOD HAS ALWAYS PUT ME IN THE POSITION THAT IF I DON'T TRUST HIM, MY FAMILY AND MYSELF WON'T MAKE IT."**

Larry Cochell promised dad that he tried to stop the firing but the Roberts were determined to get the money.

I believed he didn't have anything to do with it because he told us it wasn't right and he was going to resign over the decision. Sure enough, soon after he took another job on the west coast. Everyone thought he left for a better job because he never discussed what happened to the media.

I wanted the truth to come out but that wasn't my mom and dad's way of doing things. Letting God take care of things was always the best way.

The Bible says that "trials will come but woe to the person who brings the trials." I knew this was in God's hands. To say all this was painful and hard would be an understatement. My other son, Aaron, wasn't growing either and the doctors started running tests to see if he also had Deuschennes.

No insurance, one terminally ill child, wife who is struggling with life, and another sick kid who might have the same thing, and now we didn't have any income. Things just got harder than I could imagine.

During this time though, God was teaching me that He was my source and my shepherd. God has always put me in the position that if I don't trust Him, my family and myself won't make it. I've always faced impossible situations and God's required me to live by faith and His promises. Over the years, God's reminded me of these promises and I've held on to them, sometimes desperately.

After a couple days, I began to apply for jobs but nothing opened up. God had a different plan than one I had ever imagined. I worked for a moving company to just make some money to go along with unemployment. In the meantime, God spoke to me about working with Catholics which sounded strange and as usual, I wondered if I was just imagining things. Sure enough, I went to a Jenks High School game. There was a guy I knew that told me about two jobs available. One was at a public school and the other Monte Cassino, a catholic school. I got the job at Monte Cassino thinking it was a quick stop over to something more important, but of course, God had a different plan and boy was I wrong. Man plans his steps but God directs his path.

Cary with his "beloved" Franklin.

CHAPTER 6
Blessed by a Dog

The Lord is righteous in all his ways,
and holy in all his works. Psalm
145:17

*"Suppose God is the God you know Him to be when you are
nearest Him-what an impertinence worry is!"*

- OSWALD CHAMBERS

(Baptist Preacher and author of My Utmost for His Highest)

My time at Monte Cassino was a great experience, because of my boss named Pete Theban who was the principal, and the other teachers at the school. At a time when I needed encouragement, kindness, and understanding, he and the teachers provided it all. I taught physical education at Monte Cassino for 10 years, 9 more than what I had planned. During that time, my confidence grew and I got over a lot of my insecurities and immaturity. Pete would put me in plays where I was a two-headed beauty queen and we would sing"You Are My Sunshine" in front of the school. I was a great Tin Man and had many other opportunities to make a fool of myself while entertaining the kids. Monte Cassino wasn't really where I wanted to be but I knew it was where God wanted me. I was learning to be faithful in small things so that God would someday entrust me with much greater things.

As I look back at the 10 years at Monte Cassino, I know God was training me, disciplining me and growing me up. During this time, we got involved in the Muscular Dystrophy Association or MDA which is a great organization. Every six months, we would go to St. Louis for a research program at Barnes Hospital. It was always a good time and gave us hope with the research going on. We loved Grants Farm and the zoo, but especially the Ronald McDonald House. The boys loved all the games that were in the basement like Pac Man and Space Invaders , and I did too because It saved us money we didn't have.

I also gained perspective. Late at night, I'd help put the boys to bed, and then go to the dining room. Moms and dads would come in after long days at the hospital. They would just need to unwind while drinking coffee and sit there or sometimes talk. The stories were incredibly sad and really hard to listen to. Impossible situations for people like me to deal with. As bad as having a terminally ill son was, there were much tougher situations that I would here about and become concerned for. Sometimes we would pray together or I'd just listen and try to understand.

There was a lot of fun involved as well. We took the boys up in the Arch and it started to rain and storm which made it exciting and scary because it started to sway. Of course, I tried to scare them even more by holding them up to the windows.

I've always been a Cardinals fan ever since I listened to Bob Gibson on a transistor radio at school, strike out 17 batters to win a world series game.

RMH was sponsored by the Cardinals and they would send over free tickets for families like us. One game was the Ronald McDonald day and we happened to be the family they picked to give the tickets to. The experience included a tour of the Cardinals offices where they gave the boys a bunch of memorabilia. Next, they took us into the dugout where we got to meet and visit with Willie McGee (Cary's favorite player), Ozzie Smith and others. I enjoyed talking with the manager Whitey Herzog. The ultimate highlight was being introduced at home plate in front of thousands of fans. It was a memorable experience that our family needed and God provided.

"Cardinal fans."

One such trip, Martha and Aaron didn't come, so it was Cary and I. The first night, after I got Cary to bed at RMH, I went to the dining room and started reading my Bible in the Psalms. The passage has become God's quieting words to me. "Why art thou disquieted within me oh my soul, why art thou disquieted within me; hope thou in God." I remember thinking, that's fine Lord and I went to bed. The next day, I met with the doctors after tests were run at Barnes Hospital.

Of course, we were always expecting to hear good news about a breakthrough or new research. This time however, the news was devastating.

The doctor told me basically that Cary had no hope and that in his lifetime, there would be no cure. My heart sank like the day I found out about his Deuschennes. As I was sitting there, God spoke to me the words I'd read the night before; "Why art thou disquieted within me oh my soul, why art thou disquieted with me, hope thou in God." At that moment, I decided to trust God and rest in Him. As always, I wanted to hear from God. He was the only one who could make it alright. God was my strength and becoming more so everyday but things would not get easier. Each time Cary would have a change; legs getting weaker, starting to fall, wearing leg braces for the first time, to his first manual wheelchair and then a power wheelchair; we would go through a new grieving process. There would be denial, anger, depression and then acceptance.

> **"FRANKLIN [OUR NEW SERVICE DOG] COULD DO ANYTHING; OPEN DOORS, PICK UP PENCILS AND REMOTES, AND HE ESPECIALLY LOVED CARY. HE ALWAYS KNEW WHEN CARY WASN'T FEELING WELL BECAUSE HE WOULDN'T LEAVE HIS SIDE ON THOSE DAYS."**

My wife and I were really having trouble through it all as was to be expected. We met with our pastor and a certified counselor that went to our Church together, and after listening for an hour, they tried to tell her that the anger and unhappiness wasn't because of me or our marriage, but it was from a really hard situation that had impossible circumstances. It didn't help. She got mad and left. The counselor tried to console me and say that over 90% of marriages that lose a child end in divorce and that it was just really difficult. The pain is just too unbearable.

At this time, I was working two jobs painting houses and teaching Physical Education to pay for everything. Cary was getting weaker each year so he went from stumbling, to a push wheelchair and then into an electric wheelchair as I mentioned. When he got really weak, our insurance paid for a $17,000

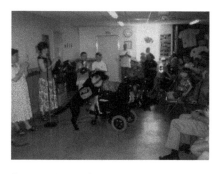

"Cary at his graduation ceremony for his service dog Franklin."

wheelchair from Sweden that changed his life. It turned on a dime and would lean back, which was a life saver because Cary couldn't hold himself up. It could travel over anything, and would even raise and lower. The insurance company was resisting but God made a way through a gentleman who was the insurance company's representative to the school. He worked hard to convince the decision makers that this particular wheelchair was needed, and he was able to make the claim go through.

There was another life changing event for our family when we were given a service dog named Franklin from a company called Therapetics that trained service dogs. Franklin was part of the first service dogs being trained in Oklahoma. It was an exciting time. Cary went from being the kid in a wheelchair to the cool kid with a fantastic dog. Cary, Franklin, and I stayed at a hotel for two weeks and trained at the Therapetics facility every day.

Franklin could do anything; open doors, pick up pencils and remotes, and he especially loved Cary. He always knew when Cary wasn't feeling well because he wouldn't leave his side on those days. Franklin would go everywhere with him—Church, school, movies and restaurants. He gave Cary confidence, love, and support that he needed at that time. I'm still amazed how God gave him the perfect dog.

Cary couldn't use his arms very well, especially late in his life and he wasn't very good at commands. The cool thing was, Franklin didn't need any of it. He was the only dog in the Therapetics program that did his own thinking. He would figure out what Cary needed without being asked. The Jenks School system put automatic doors with a big push button so Cary and Franklin didn't need any help going from building to building. Franklin would get so excited when we'd put his packs on because he knew it was time to get to work.

One of my favorite memories of Franklin was of him in Church. We'd sit close to the front with Franklin and Cary's wheelchair in the aisle. He'd fall asleep after the music every Sunday and then somehow knew when the preacher was done.

When he'd wake up, Franklin would shake like a dog does and would make a lot of noise with those packs and chain on.

I told Glenn, our preacher, that he had to pick up the energy because his boring sermons were putting my dog to sleep.

With each new circumstance of our lives, we were seeing God's care, concern, and grace interwoven in our daily activities.

It was important to count our blessings, and recognize and experience God's presence each day, so that we would know that we weren't alone and that each day held purpose and meaning. Over the next 10 years, we would experience God's grace on a daily basis and it would magnify itself as things became even more difficult.

Cary and I at grandparents.

CHAPTER 7

Working As Unto the Lord

"We labor that we may
be accepted of him."

2 Corinthians 5:9

*"The real saint is like a musician who does not need the approval
of the audience if he can catch the look of approval from His
Master (GOD)."*

- OSWALD CHAMBERS

(Noted author of My Utmost for His Highest)

God was getting me out of my comfort zone each day. School teaching was going well and I was now the athletic director for the middle school, 5th through 8th grade, which was the ages I taught also. Martha was working as a nurse, so home was good sometimes and tough sometimes.

I had gotten the idea from an add in the paper, to do sports camps in the summer which really taught me a ton. We would have 80-100 kids in all four summer camps in our small gym at Monte Cassino and I'd have 20 coaches who were usually 8th and 9th grade students I had taught. The camps would work like clock work. Mazzio's and Coca Cola were our sponsors. We'd have a Mazzio's Pizza party after camp each Friday, so they would pay for our t-shirts every year. Kids and parents would pay $5 for a pizza and pop and the party was always a great success. I'd work for a couple of months putting together prizes for the kids so that everyone went away with something as the "campers of the day."

The camps helped a ton with the bills and I was still working two jobs. Most importantly, we didn't get in debt by using credit cards or paying things off on credit. Our doctor bills were paid off consistently and it was a huge blessing to not have the added pressure of being in tremendous debt. We were just making it from month-to-month but God was faithful to provide and we were faithful to tithe to our Church each month. I knew it was important to trust God with our money because with all the doctor bills, we needed to be totally dependent upon Him.

Cary felt the most comfortable and confident in the water.

Those 10 summers were preparing me even further, though I didn't know it at the time. We'd run one basketball camp each summer, which would have 20-40 kids in it. After camp each day, I'd play one-on-one and train a kid who would help me in camp named Todd Berman. I started putting together ball handling drills, dribbling drills and scoring situations just for him. The Bible talks about small beginnings and this was the smallest, but an important step.

During this time, I could see God's hand on me but He was also very quiet like Moses in Midian, taking care of sheep. At times, it felt like God was wasting me away in a meaningless job but I was encouraged to stay faithful and keep growing. It was extremely hard though, when it seemed like everyone was mad at me at home. Cary was doing okay and we were surviving day-to-day. We started having trouble with my other son when he was 12 with school work and his attitude in general. Monte Cassino let me enroll him in school there for the 6th grade. Around the 6th and 7th grade at Monte Cassino, Aaron started having an attitude towards me of blame and resentment. In our home, my wife had made me the bad guy and the reason she was unhappy and struggling in life and Aaron started following suit with the same attitude.

One week was especially burdensome. There were now two sons in our home not doing well and a wife who was having a hard time and all of it was falling on my shoulders. Daily I would fight depression and have to work to overcome the "dark cloud" that was hovering overhead. However, one of my favorite names of God was taught to me one day when I felt the weight of the world which was "the Lifter of My Head."

"THERE WERE NOW TWO SONS IN OUR HOME NOT DOING WELL AND A WIFE WHO WAS HAVING A HARD TIME AND ALL OF IT WAS FALLING ON MY SHOULDERS."

One morning, I drove to school with Martha and Aaron both mad at me and not for any particular reason. I couldn't understand because I was working so hard to be a Godly father and husband, but nothing seemed to matter. When I got to school, I went into my office and collapsed in my chair ready to give up as so many times before. That's when God spoke to me as only He can do.

There was a calendar on my desk that's still there to this day that has Oswald Chambers quotes on it. The verse for the day was 2 Corinthians 5:9.

"We labor that we may be accepted of Him." Oswald Chambers quote under the verse said; "The real saint is like a musician who does not need the approval of the audience if he can catch the look of approval from his Master."

God knew my heart and He was telling me that He approved of me. My spirits lifted and I decided that I can't worry anymore about what others thought of me (i.e. my wife and son), but only if God was pleased with me. I felt God's pleasure on me for the first time and the love of my Heavenly Father that I needed. God didn't intend for me to live with guilt and blame through life. Instead, he wanted me to experience his favor and blessing on a daily basis. Beth Moore best explains what God was doing in my life. "We want to be overcomers with nothing to overcome. Courageous with nothing to fear. Loving with no catalyst to hate. Servants with no jerks to serve. Givers without wallets involved. Carriers of causes instead of crosses. And Jesus is way too good to let us get away with it."

Not everything was terrible or depressing though. I would have a lot of fun with the boys. I took Cary to a pro hockey game in Tulsa to watch the Roughnecks which was great until it was time to take him to the rest room. The arena didn't have a handicap bathroom so we had to go home. I had this unusual sense of humor and loved to tease and mess with the boys. We would stop on trips and I'd go in and order sandwiches at Subway. About halfway through the sandwich, I'd hear the boys start yelling at me because somehow jalapeños would end up in the middle of the sandwich. One Christmas, I wrapped up presents for the boys that had women's garments in them.

Aaron thought Cary's hose and bra were real funny until he got the same thing.

I used to tell Cary that it must be a wonderful thing to have such a great looking father. As serious as only Cary could get, he cautiously and tastefully informed me that I really wasn't that good looking. Then he tried to make up for it and reassure me that I wasn't too bad though. From anyone else, my feelings would have been hurt but I couldn't get mad at Cary. When I would get frustrated or upset at him, he would apologize and I'd feel guilty for a week and work hard to make it up to him.

We were able to buy this really cool van where Cary's wheelchair would automatically lock into the floor of the van and the sliding door would also open with the push of a button. One day while visiting parents and grandparents, we took a trip up the Arbuckle Mountains. I couldn't help myself. Cary and Aaron were right by the automatic door and halfway up the mountain, I drove real close to the side and strategically started to open the door. By the time I got the door back closed, the boys were yelling and griping at me. It was worth all the abuse of course.

Happy Days.

CHAPTER 8

Angelic Road Side Assistance

"With God all things are possible."

Matthew 19:26

"When Jesus asks us what we want Him to do for us in regard to the incredible thing with which we are faced, remember that He does not work in common-since ways, but in supernatural ways. If it is an impossibility, it is the thing we have to ask. God will do the absolutely impossible."

OSWALD CHAMBERS

(Baptist preacher and noted author)

There was never any doubt that God was watching over my family because He would reassure me in so many ways. My prayers have always been straight forward and to the point, believing the verse, "You have not because you ask not." We were driving a very small Honda that barely carried anything besides our family. Cary was now in his wheelchair and we had no way to transport it. We were driving a small car because a family that had a lot of money (i.e. big house, nice cars), sold us a lemon that kept blowing head gaskets. My mechanic from Church said the owner knew it was a bad car. Always wondered how the man reaped what he sowed since he took advantage of a vulnerable young family.

That was the money we had used from selling our house in Bethany, about $5,000, when we moved to Tulsa. With the money we had left from the move, we were able to buy a small Honda for around $1,200.

As I always do, I began to pray that God would somehow supply us with a car so that we could transport Cary's wheelchair around to places. A couple weeks later, I was driving my old truck down Lewis, coming home from school and an elderly lady didn't see me and smacked me pretty good on the side. It totaled my old truck but it also gave me whiplash in my neck and low back. Both started bothering me, so I went to a chiropractor who I had heard on the radio named Ivan Bebermeyer who also became a good friend. His office manager, who he fired later, tried to get me to sue the driver and the insurance company for everything they have which I wouldn't do. Her insurance company did however, pay for my doctor bills and they also settled with me for $10,000 for pain and suffering. We were able to take the money and buy a used Mercury Sable station wagon that was perfect for my family. From now on, I could throw the light wheelchair in the back of that wagon a couple thousand times over the years.

My family was really struggling one time and I began to pray that God would somehow allow us to go on a vacation or something, to help us get out of the depression and out from under the dark cloud. A couple of weeks later, two families (each by themselves) from school without ever talking to me, submitted my son's name to the Make a Wish foundation. Monte Cassino let us leave school early in May for Disney World for seven days and six nights for a wonderful trip that we needed very much. God had once again provided. The boys were around 8 and 10 at the time and couldn't have been happier.

My son loved Michael Jordan at the time. Being a former basketball player and playing in leagues for ten years, Cary would watch games with me. I began to pray as usual, that God would somehow allow us to meet Michael Jordan, or something; I didn't really know what to ask for. Two weeks later, I got a call at home from a company that I didn't know of. They asked me if my son liked Michael Jordan. I never told anyone about my prayers for the vacation or Michael Jordan.

Of course I said yes. The gentleman then informed me that his company wanted to send Cary and I to Chicago to watch Michael Jordan and the Bulls play the Milwaukee Bucks. We were seated on the front row and got waited on by pretty girls which I enjoyed teasing my son about. The game had lot's

"Cary on the front row of the Bulls game."

of excitement with Dennis Rodman getting thrown out and throwing his jersey to a lady in the second deck. Cary couldn't understand why a lady went crazy when she caught the Rodman jersey but we enjoyed the whole experience. God always knew how to refresh and restore our souls and lead us beside still waters.

We needed to buy an electric wheelchair because Cary was getting weaker which also meant we needed to purchase a used van to accommodate his wheelchair. It was too heavy to put in the station wagon we had and too big.

After purchasing a nice used van, we were coming home one night, (remember we didn't have cell phones) on I-44 between Oklahoma City and Tulsa, we blew a tire in the middle of nowhere. Aaron was around 10 and Cary, who couldn't walk, was about 12. As I went to change the tire, there wasn't a jack. My heart sank. It was pitch black outside. Of course, I began to pray an impossible prayer and a car pulled up, didn't say a word to me and proceeded to change the tire. After finishing, the man jumped back in their car, still without saying or acknowledging us, and drove away. I don't know what an angel looks like, but I'd bet my farm that's who it was.

Each time we were hurting for money, God would provide. When we lost our job at ORU, our preacher at Church took another job and he asked us to stay in their nice house for free and to repair what needed fixing, like the deck and do upkeep. Another great answer to prayer. When our preacher sold his house, friends from Church took a job in New York and needed someone to live in their house.

They only charged us $200 a month and since I did a lot of work on the house and yard without being asked, they didn't charge us some months because they said God told them not to.

One month, we were really hurting for money, with doctor bills and expenses pilling up and I was working two jobs still. At one job site I was painting by myself, in an old abandoned house. It was in bad shape and no one had lived there for a few years. One day, I opened a small door in the ceiling, a crawl hole, and $1700 fell out and landed on me. Still don't know how to explain it but "God."

Couple of years after going to Disneyworld, I began to pray the same prayer that God would allow us to go on a vacation, some kind of a getaway or something. Sure enough, an organization that I wasn't familiar with, called me out of the blue and asked if we would like to go to Disneyworld. They were just like Make a Wish, but not as well known. The trip was perfect: everything from the limo ride to the airport, to staying at the Disney World resort for handicap kids where Mickey Mouse, Donald Duck, and others would visit the lunch and breakfast hall everyday. My favorite part was the free ice cream shed by our duplex that was open to guests every day.

The only bad experience I had was the Black Mountain Roller Coaster, a ride inside of a mountain, which I actually thought was sort of slow. I was terrified the whole time, wondering if Cary's head was crashing against the sides, and until it was over, I couldn't get to him. He was fine and just laughed at me for being scared.

As bad as that was, the trip was exactly what we needed. God has always been intricately and strategically involved in our lives. There were so many other times where God would answer a prayer as only He could. Always with perfect timing and the perfect answer to my prayers. Every good and perfect gift is from above. The Bible says deep calls unto deep. The depth of our pain and struggle was met by a grace that took care of every need and would give peace to my soul. The pain, at times, would make me numb, but I'd find solace in my times of talking to God and letting Him raise me up and set me on higher and level ground to stabilize me. He'd do that with encouraging words and promises.

I didn't pray much for peace, patience, contentment and the like! I needed real substance. Things, like sleep, stress to be relieved, money for bills and my sons to be ok. The more I prayed and read my Bible though, I found peace, joy, love and contentment. I even found love for someone who didn't love me. God was encouraging, but also tough on me when I wouldn't do the right thing or treat Martha with anything but kindness and love. The standard I held up for Cary, that even though you have a disease, you still have to do the right thing, that was even more true for me and it was a constant conviction; I have no excuse to not do the right thing.

God has always protected me from wandering eyes and a wandering heart which I'm thankful for because I know I was extremely vulnerable. His grace was always sufficient.

Our Second Trip to Disney World.
The Disney characters were a lot of fun at the Disney Complex.

CHAPTER 9
God sent Bugs to Bring Her Back

"I am the vine; ye are the branches."

John 15:5

"Are you prepared to let God take you into union with Himself, and pay no more attention to what you call the "important things?" Are you prepared to abandon entirely and let go?"

OSWALD CHAMBERS

(Noted author and preacher)

I'm still not sure how you handle an angry and depressed wife or a rebellious son or a dying child, but I do know what it included.

God didn't give me work to get lost in, or friends to be close to, even though I had a couple Godly friends, what could they really do to help? I know it was on purpose. He wanted me to depend totally on Him as my source and supply. I needed to know God was my righteousness, because I was being told I wasn't enough. God needed to become the "Lifter of my Head" because I was constantly fighting discouragement. Each day, I needed Jehovah Jireh (my provider) because we were in need of so much. God became my shepherd because I was lost and confused by the struggles. I needed Jehovah Shamah, Hebrew word for "Jehovah is there" because I felt so alone all the time. And God really had to be Jehovah Rophe meaning "I am the Lord that healeth thee" because we needed healing in so many ways. God was forcing me or giving me the opportunity, however you think your Bible defines it, to depend upon Him. There had to be a selling out of everything on Him; either I was going to be a complete failure or God was going to show Himself mighty on my behalf. I'm either going to be a fool, I told God, or He's going to have to come through for me. There were glimpses of God's glory but I wanted so much more.

> **"I'M EITHER GOING TO BE A FOOL, I TOLD GOD, OR HE'S GOING TO HAVE TO COME THROUGH FOR ME."**

At one point, because I was constantly being told I wasn't enough and it appeared I was always failing, I made a list of everything I could think of, or find that God says about me and that I knew to be true. It's a long list but it was very important for my encouragement and survival. I keep the list in my safe to this day as a reminder. It went like this; I am: Salt of the earth, Light of the world, Loved by God, Called to Be a Saint, Now under no condemnation, Co-Heirs with Christ, More Than a Conquerer, New Creation, Righteousness of God, Crucified with Christ, a Son, Redeemed through His blood, Alive with Christ, Seated with Christ in Heavenly realms,

God's Workmanship, Created for Good Works, Strong in
the Lord, Fullness in Christ, Chosen, Holy, Dearly Loved, Like
Christ in Love, Recipient of Abundant Grace, Justified.

Then God, like He always does, challenged me even
further. Martha was at an all time low and I wasn't any help
because of her distrust of me.

She had some horrible experiences before we were
married that made it tough for her to relate to me. It wasn't
her fault. She was hurting as much as me.

One day out of the blue, Martha left! She was planning,
I think, on being gone for good because she signed a 6
month lease for an apartment. She left me with the boys,
a full-time job and everything that includes. I knew it was
all she could do to cope at the time. She was angry at God,
but knew that wasn't right, so being angry and blaming
me helped her to stay out of depression as my preacher
and psychiatrist explained it to Martha and I. To say I was
overwhelmed all of a sudden would be an understatement,
but God as always reassured me in Psalm 34:6. "This poor
man cried, and the Lord heard him, and saved him out of all
his troubles." Trusting God to take care of the situation was
becoming normal but not easy.

That week, I was finishing up painting a house. Still
remember some guys from Church and my pastor coming
over to help me finish the job, which was huge because I
was overwhelmed to say the least. Cary needed constant
care and Aaron was still young, so I'd get up at dawn and go
to bed after midnight. Again I was numb and remember
thinking "what am I going to do?" Martha would visit the

boys to say hello, but that was about it. In my lowest, my Pastor Glenn was over at my house late one evening after I got the boys to bed and he asked me a question that has defined my life. My name, Donald. means "overcomer" and God has given me the blessing and pleasure to overcome, becoming broken bread and poured out wine for His Purposes. Glenn asked me, "If this is what it takes for God to get me where He wants, is that ok?," I thought for awhile and responded with a confident yes. Remember, I had decided to sell out to God. After Glenn left, I prayed "God, whatever comes, it's ok because it's you I want and you are enough." A peace came over me that carried me through and helped me as always to overcome.

God also gave me the grace to love Martha and to love her like Christ loved the Church, which was to die to myself. I chose instead to not fight, accuse or blame but decided to treat her with love and respect. Slowly, God changed her heart. It was around Christmas and I surprised her when she came over to see the boys, giving her a beautiful leather coat. Soon after that, I helped her get out of the lease because there were tons of bugs in her apartment and she couldn't live there. One thing I've learned (and God would remind me of frequently) is that He is always at work. His ways are not our

"AS ALWAYS, THE BOYS AND I WOULD MAKE THE MOST OF THINGS BECAUSE I GENUINELY ENJOYED HAVING FUN WITH THEM. THEY MADE EVERYTHING BETTER."

ways and I was learning that His ways are right and perfect, timely and always best. Leave it to God to use bugs to accomplish His purposes; as He did use locusts and donkeys in the Bible before.

Glenn was preaching one Sunday and he was saying that God would get your attention usually in one of three ways; your family, your finances, or your health. After the sermon, I went up front and asked Glenn what it meant if all three were a mess. We both laughed and he said "I guess he's really trying to get your attention." I was dead serious, but I laughed anyway.

My sister Deana and I, had this running joke about how people would always say you are so strong, not knowing that I was dying on the inside. Deana was going through her own nightmare. When we'd hang up on the phone with each other, we'd give our well known quips for encouragement such as: take it easy, keep your head up, stay strong, glad your doing so well and many others. People meant well, but had no idea how hard life was from day-to-day. I know I keep saying this but things were getting ready to get even tougher. Anyone who believes that God doesn't give us more than we can handle, hasn't read the Bible carefully enough. Whether it was Paul, Moses, Abraham or Joseph, God always puts us in the position that apart from Him, we are going to fail. My job was to live obediently, in worship and praise of Him.

As always, the boys and I would make the most of things because I genuinely enjoyed having fun with them. They made everything better. I would set the boys at the counter and start dinner with them watching and show off as if

I was a great cook. Actually, I was horrible, like the time I put the corn in the wrong bowl on the oven and it broke into a number of pieces and the corn went everywhere. Cary laughed so hard his stomach hurt and Aaron in his sweet voice asked, "Is everything okay dad?"The boys and I would get a reprieve during the week though. On Mondays, we'd eat at Pizza Hut because kids under a certain age ate free and then on Tuesdays, we'd eat at Rex's Chicken, also enjoying the boys eating free. We'd have fun while stuffing ourselves.

The boys and I would go on a trip to Mountain View, Oklahoma to visit my parents and grandparents, which is farming country. The last couple hours of the trip, I'd try to convince them that the cows were fake statues that farmers would put out to trick city folks and that the horses were mechanical machines that would just walk back and forth. We would play the alphabet game and I'd make up words which the boys would call me on but they didn't know for sure so I'd give my best argument. There was always some kind of fun going on.

Reunion picture of the Thunder vs. Trailblazers game in 2014 with Terry Stolts & Al Beal. Terry is smiling because Portland had just beaten OKC.

CHAPTER 10
New Beginnings From Being Fired

"God is our refuge and strength, a
very present help in trouble."

Psalm 46:1

*"Faith is robust, vigorous confidence built on the fact that God is
holy love. You cannot see Him just now, you cannot understand
what He is doing but you know Him."*

OSWALD CHAMBERS

(Baptist preacher and author)

After being at Monte Cassino for 9 years, I started
coaching again, mainly because I was bored to death. The
8th grade team I coached did ok and I enjoyed it. The next
year, my tenth, the team I coached was put in the Tulsa City
league with the really good teams instead of the Catholic
League, which had only pretty weak teams.

This was important because the year before, one
of my students dad's was a majority owner of a sports
complex called Champions. Doctor Richard Ranne asked
me if I'd be interested in doing some basketball lessons
at Champions after school and on Saturdays. Sounded
good to me, so I told him I'd think about it. Instead, I asked

some kids at school and parents if I'd offer some lessons at Monte Cassino, would they be interested. My schedule was full by the end of the week. It was something I loved doing and was actually pretty good at. Training Todd in previous summers, was a big help because I just continued where I had dropped off from him. He gave me someone to experiment on.

That next year was when I had Dr. Ranne's son, Jason on my team as well as some other good players. We won our division and so I was chosen to coach the all-star team with three of our players, since we had won, and two players from the other teams. We practiced at Monte Cassino all week and the players indicated to me that these were the first "real practices" they had participated in and they really enjoyed themselves.

Of course, we blew out the other division all star team. After the game, a few of the players came up and asked me if I'd help them get on an AAU team, so I got all their numbers and promised to call them next week.

The game got me thinking, why not coach the team? So I gave Dr. Ranne a call and gave him a proposal that if he'd take care of everything; money, travel, uniforms etc, I'd coach the team. He agreed and was excited. That first year, we won every tournament and only lost a couple games. The competition wasn't great because we were just figuring out what tournaments to participate in. Something important happened though; we became really good friends. He would call me or I'd call him many times during the week.

A lot of times, he'd be in surgery and the nurse would hold the phone for him which was very interesting.

This habit of calling, especially late at night, would prove to be a God send a few years later.

Dr. Ranne again asked me to start doing some lessons at Champions and this time, I agreed. The Bible, as I mentioned, talks about small beginnings and the size of a mustard seed (Zechariah 4:10) and of course, this was very small and I had no idea where it was going. I'd get off work at school and drive 30 minutes to Champions and do lessons until 9pm.

Early on, God made a covenant with me, that if I wouldn't do lessons on Sunday and stay faithful, that He would bless my small business. Being naive at this point, I said yes not knowing how binding and tempting it would be. Over the years, I could have made a ton of money on Sundays, but there was no way I was breaking that agreement. Knowing that if I wanted God's favor, that Sunday was my day of rest and that no matter what, God would always get the first fruits of the money.

"I'VE ALWAYS HAD A HEALTHY FEAR OF GOD. MARTHA GOT MAD AT ME A COUPLE TIMES WHEN I TITHED BECAUSE WE REALLY NEEDED THE MONEY, BUT I TRUSTED GOD ALWAYS TO PROVIDE AND HE DID, EVERY TIME."

Martha got mad at me a couple times when I tithed because we really needed the money, but I trusted God always to provide and he did. Every time.

Lessons were going well, the AAU team was off and running and it was the end of my tenth year at Monte Cassino. Every year in May, Sr. Mary Claire, who was the school administrator and Pete Theban, the middle school principal and usually one other person, would meet with each teacher and offer a salary for the next year and talk about what was coming up for the new year. My meeting was that next morning and as was my custom, I was reading my Bible that night. God impressed on me the importance of trusting Him in every circumstance and that change was

coming. As I was driving to school the next morning, there was a huge billboard that said that change was coming. Now God had my attention.

"St. Francis Hawks winning the AAU national Championship tournament."

When I got to school and went to the meeting room, everyone was very quiet which was unusual. Sr. Mary Claire went on to say that with all the struggles, they thought it would be better if I would move on. I'm sure that I wasn't the same person who had been teaching there for 10 years. The constant worry, lack of sleep, and a growing discontent with wanting to move on with bigger and better things, was showing up in my everyday life and teaching.

However, they were going to pay for my salary the next 6 months and cover our insurance, which we had to have, for the next year and a half.

God had graciously prepared me as He always had, to trust him because He's Jehovah Jireh, our provider. I went away from the meeting somewhat in shock, but I was also excited for what God had planned.

When I got home and told Martha what happened, she let me have it. Trying to explain to her how God had encouraged me and had a plan, didn't help at all and just made her more mad. I was again a failure in her eyes and as always, was doing a sorry job providing for our family. My faith was being tested again through family and finances and as always, health.

John Piper, a well known Baptist preacher and author says: "We think we know how to do something big and God makes it big. Barren Sarah gives birth to the child of promise. Gideon's 300 men defeat one hundred thousand Midianites. A slingshot in the hands of a shepherd boy brings the giant down. A virgin bears the Son of God. A boy's five loaves feed thousands. A breach of justice, groveling political expediency and criminal torture on a gruesome cross become the foundation of the salvation of the world. This is God's way-to take all the boasting off of man and put it on God." There definitely wouldn't be any boasting on my part.

Cary with Franklin and Binky.

CHAPTER 11

Fighting through the Mental Cobwebs

"He that dwelleth in the secret place of the most High shall abide under the shadow of the Almighty."

Psalm 91:1

"When we live in the secret place of prayer it becomes impossible for us to doubt God. We become more sure of Him than of anything else."

OSWALD CHAMBERS

(Author and Baptist preacher)

There were times in my life when I was fearless and confident, especially on the basketball court. Most of the time however, I wasn't. One of the reasons we work on kids insecurities so much in our camps is because I know how it hurts and hinders someone like myself. God had to really grow me in this area. Left brain kids or kids with the engineer type brain especially have to work on their ability to overcome fear of failure and fear of rejection. What I learned was that as long as I worried about what others thought, I couldn't enjoy life or accomplish my best because it's a huge burden to have this anchor or albatross around my neck.

I call it living with cobwebs. Cobwebs make the path unclear, suspicious, or fearful of what's ahead. They make you hesitant and worrisome if not taken care of. How do you take care of your cobwebs? Through the Words of God and the testimony of who you are in Christ. Jesus will never reject me, I don't have to earn his love or care. He will never forsake me. There's never a time or situation that he's not in control. Every situation is for my good and His glory. Trials and hard times will come but never without his consent and presence in the midst of them. Cobwebs distort that. It makes you ponder the "what if." I won't go take a shot, because I might miss. I don't go drive the ball because I might turn it over.

"JESUS WILL NEVER REJECT ME, I DON'T HAVE TO EARN HIS LOVE OR CARE. HE WILL NEVER FORSAKE ME. THERE'S NEVER A TIME OR SITUATION THAT HE'S NOT IN CONTROL."

All basketball terms I know, but it means you might fail. Every basketball player interviewed at half time or after the game, whatever the interviewer asks will be answered with "I just wanted to stay aggressive." What they are saying is they need to clear out the cobwebs. Cobwebs build up. They don't go away with time, only effort and work. I had to get to work. When you don't have cobwebs you see a pretty girl and you ask her out instead of pondering her "no" or rejection.

If I see a job I want, I go nail the interview and go for it instead of pondering whether he/she will like me or not, or if I will measure up.

I always wanted to be great at something but I've learned that you never exceed physically where you are mentally/emotionally. This is true on the basketball floor, in the workplace, and even in marriage.

Satan causes confusion, insecurity, blame and excuses. All of this is cobwebs. God was very clear with me: obey and trust. I had to clear out my own cobwebs so that he could lead me wherever he wanted me to go and do whatever he wants me to do. This all sounds easy and at times I've mastered it. Other times I've been led by fear and trembling, but still led somehow by God's grace. Other times, I've totally blown it and God would graciously get me back on track. I haven't mastered cobwebs but, my mind is clear now most of the time because wherever God leads, I'm ready to go. Clear path ahead, ready to follow, sometimes kicking and screaming but never doubting. So whether my wife, boss, or coach is happy with me or mad and disappointed in me, it doesn't change how I think of myself and whether I'm going to do the right thing.

My mind is clear: trust and obey. There are still things to this day that if God doesn't come through, I'm going to fail miserably. God is most offended by my unbelief. Even writing this book, he's had to remind me that it's not my job to worry about what happens with it, only to write it. As always, it's like "Okay, God, I understand the lesson one more time." Fear and worry is a conversation you have with yourself that causes stress and health problems and it exacerbates things; whereas prayer is a conversation you have with God that changes your heart and your disposition.

The boys and I with Mark Price in the hotel before the Dallas Mavericks versus Cleveland Cavaliers Game.

CHAPTER 12
God never uses a Man Greatly until He hurts Him Deeply

"The Lord is my rock, and my fortress, and my deliverer; my God, my strength, in whom I will trust; my buckler, and the horn of my salvation, and my high tower."

Psalm 18:2

"We act like pagans in a crisis, only one out of a crowd is daring enough to bank his faith in the character of God."

OSWALD CHAMBERS

(Baptist preacher and author)

The next day after getting fired, I got to work on "Score" in faith. There was no other choice or backup plan. Looking back, it was perfect. God gave me six months to get this small business going. A friend of mine came up with the name Score Basketball and helped me design my first brochure.

Being determined, I'm glad I didn't know at the time that 90% of businesses fail, 80% in the first two years. The lessons took place in one of the two gyms until the adult leagues would start and then we moved upstairs where Dr. Ranne put in a portable goal for me.

It was a terrible place to give lessons but surprisingly, students and parents didn't seem to mind. Because the upstairs was on concrete, my back would start bothering me by the end of the day. Slowly but surely, the schedule started filling up. Champions didn't provide any advertisement but Dr. Ranne did help me put up a cool sign and display in the front of Champions.

Over the years, and especially early on, I'd try everything; camps, clinics, advertising, brochures to schools, on cars and to businesses and anything else I could think of. Slowly, I started putting together different skill sets such as fourteen different slides, twenty-five different moves, six ball handling series and 30 different jumpers to work on and over 50 different dribbling drills. Now there are eighteen different areas that we train and develop in. It was all coming together.

Dr. Ranne knew I couldn't stay upstairs much longer and grow, so the board at Champions decided to close the baseball batting machines and build a third gym just for Score. After that, my schedule filled up quickly, especially on Saturdays. Lessons could go from 8am to 6pm. At first, I only did individual lessons but soon started doing group classes, shooting classes and weight lifting classes as well. Everyday, there was a ton to do because I was taking care of everything myself: the books, advertisement, collections, taxes, cleaning, equipment and everything you could think of. The gym started looking pretty good as I put up banners, pictures, posters and marking boards with all kinds of inspirational messages I believed in. Eventually, Champions built me an office in the corner of the gym.

It was just a black chained link fence that was about fifteen feet tall but I liked it a lot.

Finally, Score had a place to lock everything up and I actually had a desk to work off of. Getting a cell phone for the first time also helped and I would get calls constantly. Score was at the perfect place to begin a business. Every kid that played AAU would play in tournaments at Champions and would come over and watch the lessons. They'd only have to watch for a few minutes to get interested. It's amazing, as I look back, how God worked everything out for Score to grow and be successful. I worked hard but I knew it was because of

> **"FINALLY, SCORE HAD A PLACE TO LOCK EVERYTHING UP AND ACTUALLY HAD A DESK TO WORK OFF OF."**

God's favor and blessing everyday that made it work. I was thankful for the daily encouragement and promises that God would give me.

After ORU, my father took a high school job back at his home town of Mountain View, Oklahoma as the basketball coach and principal. A few years later, he moved on to Caprock High School in Amarillo, Texas which was a smart move because when he was able to retire, he had double the retirement pay from Oklahoma and Texas.

While dad was in Caprock, I helped him train his team a couple times. Once when I was there, Denny Price, father of NBA players Mark and Brent, stopped by to visit Dad and sat in on my training. When I got back to Tulsa, he came by and watched me train some more players. A couple of weeks later, he called me up one morning and we talked for a couple of hours. He wanted to know everything about Score and what my training was all about because he was considering starting his own program in Enid, Oklahoma where he was coaching at a small college there. Shortly after this, he wrote me a letter telling me I was the best trainer he had ever watched train. This coming from a guy who coached in the NBA and who NBA teams hired to train players to shoot. God was building my confidence and I appreciated the letter.

Mom always felt bad about not being able to help much with Cary over the years, but she and dad made up for it when he retired early and they moved back to Tulsa around 2000. Dad and Mom trusted me so I bought their house for them by just showing them pictures and signing all of the paperwork for them.

Later on, Dad became the manager of Champions for a couple of years and I got him to coach an AAU team of girls that I was training and he did a great job and won most of the tournaments, including the National AAU Invitational tournament. A couple of years later, Dad started getting the shakes and having some weakness in his legs. He was diagnosed with Parkinson's shortly after that. My strong active father was headed for a difficult life. It was a great time having Dad at Champions for a couple years but Mom and Dad's life was getting ready to change drastically.

When I was in college, I went and heard a speaker at the Baptist Student Union named Peter Lord. He preached

on "What is, Is." He was such a great speaker that I bought
a series he recorded on "Fear" that God would use to help
change my life. While painting a house one summer, I'd start
painting early in the morning and listen to these cassette
tapes all day. God was renewing my mind and training me
to think with a Godly perspective. The impact these tapes
had on me can't be overstated. I know, because they helped
change my whole way of thinking.

The tapes covered
everything from my insecurities
to my fear of failure, fear of
rejection and every fear that
you could imagine.

God was taking away
Satan's ammunition against
me in every trial and difficult
situation. Peter Lord helped

"The boys and I at Sea World."

give me the tools to live by faith and not by fear. Score
became a combination of hard work and faith. Once during
practice at Oklahoma University, a guy dove on the floor with
no chance to save the ball because he was out of control,
and coach used the analogy of a war movie to make his
point. He gave the example of how in war movie battles,
there was always 10-20 guys that would go running into
enemy fire knowing they had no chance to stay alive. He told
us to dive for the ball, but to stay alive. "Let the other guy die
for his country" he said.

I remembered this analogy one time when I was talking to God (probably arguing was more like it), that if Cary had to die "for his country," then it needed to be for a good reason, not some "he lived a tough life and that is it." It needs to be for earth shattering reasons.

As basketball training and Score was growing and developing, family life would only get even more difficult. Watching my family struggle through life, especially Cary, would only test my faith. From my fathers Parkinsons, to developing Score, to finding meaning and purpose in Cary's life, faith was required at every turn. On one hand, I was looking forward to what God had planned, but dreading the inevitable at times. The answer was in allowing God to renew my mind daily and living in thankfulness, forgiveness and faith. Sounds easy now, but it took God's grace everyday.

Joni Eareckson Tada, a quadraplegic who is an author, artist, radio host, and founder of Joni and Friends wrote my favorite book about Heaven (*Heaven, Your Real Home*) that I really needed to assure me that Cary dying wasn't the worst thing in life, only momentary affliction. Like Cary, she took away my excuses for a bad attitude to complain, or to pity myself, or to not expect the best of people, or to treat people right no matter how they'd treat me.

I love books and movies about redeeming value, comeback stories, and people overcoming. I'll watch the same movies over and over because they inspire me as I see individuals overcoming great odds. Movies like *Instinct* with Anthony Hopkins, or *Sea Biscuit*, *Iron Will*, *Family Man*, *Count of Monte Cristo*, or *Man Without a Face*. These are stories about men or women who may have struggled in life, had unthinkable tragedies, or maybe even blew it in some big way. But who had a comeback and overcame these great odds that defined their life as being worth every battle, every heartache and every struggle. Joni Eareckson Tada inspired me to see everything as a blessing and something to be embraced and thankful for, even if it meant having to go through hard times.

I heard a sermon by Life Action Ministries one time, where the preacher said that "God never uses a man greatly until he hurts them deeply." That sounds harsh but it's the life of a Christian if you want to add redeeming value to others and for God to do great things through you. God makes all things new but he does it through struggles, heartache and sometimes loss. I'm afraid, as people we have become the example where it talks about the end times in the Bible, where we will be lovers of self and lovers of pleasure. If God was to use me greatly, a life of hardship needed to be okay with me. That doesn't mean there won't be great times or that I would choose the hardship, but that in the midst of the hardship, I would be all in to worship God in struggles, rejoice in pain and to be

"GOD NEVER USES A MAN GREATLY UNTIL HE HURTS THEM DEEPLY."

thankful in all things. If that wasn't the outcome, the time isn't redeemed. God will make the most of every tear, every heartache, every struggle; it just takes faith.

Not a faith where everything is going to be great or that healing will come, relationships restored, all the money I need, or even great success, but a faith that Heaven is for real and that my time on earth is just temporary and my reward is being laid up for me to be received one day and the reason I was created would be fulfilled.

> "IF CHRIST WOULD COME TO EARTH TO DIE FOR ME, THEN TO FOLLOW HIM I MUST BE WILLING TO DIE TO MYSELF. A DEAD MAN ISN'T OFFENDED, A DEAD MAN ISN'T CONCERNED ABOUT WHAT OTHERS THINK OR SAY, A DEAD MAN DOESN'T CONSIDER HIS OWN NEEDS ABOVE OTHERS, A DEAD MAN DOESN'T WORRY ABOUT THE FUTURE."

Reaping what I sowed became what I counted on. God loves to give and he lives to bless, but most importantly, He wants a relationship with me and He wants me to grow into the image of Jesus Christ so that one day I could be like Paul; a servant of Christ who was broken bread and poured out wine for God's great purposes. What became clear to me was that there was no greater calling than to be used by Christ to help others know Him. If Christ would come to earth to die for me, then to follow Him I must be willing to die to myself. A dead man isn't offended, a dead man isn't concerned about what others think or say, a dead man doesn't consider his own needs above others, a dead man doesn't worry about the future.

A dead man doesn't consider his own rights above others or even take advantage of his rights. Instead, he allows God to choose for him whether good or bad, mistreated or not, or think of himself more highly than others. To live as a dead man, that meant Christ could live in me, and I knew He could do much greater things Himself than I ever could. Who would have thought Joni Eareckson Tada would inspire millions to follow Jesus Christ? What an incredible redeeming life she has lived. There are no cobwebs in her life. She is focused, determined and committed to living her life for Jesus Christ and to follow him at all cost.

My AAU basketball team helped provide a great distraction at times from the inevitable. Martha and the boys went on a couple of trips with the team when they could and Dr. Ranne would take care of everything. Our team was really good. We won most tournaments and would blow teams out by 30-50 points. When games would get out of hand, a couple of guys on the team, Matt and Marcus usually, would start coaching for me without asking of course. They would do their best "Coach Calvert" impression, drinking out of my water bottle, throwing my clip board and even calling timeouts to yell at players.

This is the same Matt and Marcus that I would give a ride to practice in my bright yellow Ford truck. One time, I honked at someone I recognized on the sidewalk and both guys ducked under the dash and said "Coach, you know we are in a yellow truck, correct?" The players were bragging on their shoes one day after practice in our end-of-practice huddle at mid-court.

I informed the players that I only paid $40 for my basketball shoes and they all looked at them and said "Coach, we know!" Of course everyone broke up laughing.

More than one time, one of the black guys on the team, usually Ralph Charles who played at Oral Roberts University or Matt Berry who played at Indiana State, would receive an alley-oop from Cedrick or David. Meanwhile Patrick Nally, our non-jumping white center walked under the side basket headed to the bench to change shoes, and Ralph or Matt would proceed to dunk on Patrick and land on his shoulders, thereby "posterizing him" as players would say.

Sometimes in practice, I'd have my point guards practice throwing alley oops or throwing over the top against defenses to our big guys at the rim which, were about 6'-3" to 6'-6" black guys that could really jump, except for Patrick, our aforementioned talented white center who played football at Notre Dame but couldn't jump two inches off the floor. One day, all of the black guys were in the front of the line and guards threw perfect passes to the front of the rim and players would either dunk the ball or lay it in over the rim. When Patrick came up to receive his pass, Jesse McNeal threw the ball towards the bottom of the net on purpose and every player on the team, except Patrick, fell to the floor laughing so hard, we had to stop practice for awhile.

We had a guy on our team, Jessie, that would always butt heads with me, but I loved him because he was a fighter. He took it personal if we were getting beat or if someone scored on him. I love the saying "It's easier to quiet the fanatic than to raise the dead."

My college coach, Dave Bliss, once told me that every team needs a kamikaze guy. Someone who, when the game wasn't going well, could come in and create havoc for the other team. That was Jesse. His high school coach didn't like him or utilize him very much because he would question and argue. I actually liked it most of the time. At times, it kept us on edge when needed. I always wanted my players to "own the team" and take responsibility for our winning and losing. I'd ask them questions at time outs and ask what match-ups to exploit or changes to make.

Interesting note though— Jesse could argue with me but no one, not on our team, could. He was fiercely loyal and would attack referees for me, or opposing coaches. One time before a game in Wichita Kansas, a lady got mad at our team because she couldn't see and she proceeded to attack me for no reason. I started to say something and Jesse said "I got this coach." Jesse quickly put her in her place and let her know not to talk to our coach that way.

"EVERY TEAM NEEDS A KAMIKAZE GUY. SOMEONE, WHEN THE GAME WASN'T GOING WELL COULD COME IN AND CREATE HAVOC FOR THE OTHER TEAM."

"Jason Ranne shooting a jumpshot at The Wide World of Sports Complex at Disney World during the National AAU Tournament."

One very rewarding consequence of coaching this team was from having Jason Ranne on the team. He went on to play for the Arizona Wildcats who made it to the Final Four his freshman year. Jason's dad, Dr. Ranne, flew me all over the country with himself to see Arizona play, including the Final Four for the week. I got to see them play LSU in Louisiana and Purdue at the Indiana Pacers Coliseum and the University of Illinois in the Great 8 in San Antonio, before heading to the Final Four in Minneapolis, Minnesota.

I have so many important memories of this team because they gave me so much reprieve from the darkest of days. God would bless me with such joy and excitement that started with a little all-star team. God is always perfect with His ways and gifts.

Score Basketball Camps are Always Packed.

CHAPTER 13

The Man Who Saved my Son

"This is the victory that overcometh
the world, even our faith."

1 John 5:4

*"Faith must be tested, because it can be turned into a personal
possession only through conflict."*

OSWALD CHAMBERS

(Baptist Preacher and author)

My business was going well and so was my AAU team.
Basketball couldn't have been any better. However, Aaron
was having lots of trouble in school and was struggling
attitude—wise as well. I didn't know it at the time, but he
started smoking marijuana and hanging out with the wrong
crowd. Watching his brother waste away was getting more
difficult for him every year. The start of marijuana and what
that entails, would lead him down a path that would take
him years to recover from.

My AAU team, called the St. Francis Hawks, finished up
201-18 in four years and we had won numerous tournaments
and a couple of national championships. I had trained four
NBA players and helped numerous players go play at places
like Arizona, Kansas, Kentucky, Georgia, ORU, Oklahoma

State University, Indiana State, and many more. None of this mattered in 1998 because we were losing Cary. He was getting so weak that our primary care doctor, Dr. Mays, informed us one day that he had 48 hours to live.

What I didn't mention is that Dr. Ranne is a pediatric surgeon. He would call late at night to check in on the team, see how things were going and ask what the schedule looked like for the weekend. Cary would always talk to Rick and ask him questions to check on him like, "how was he feeling or if he was working too hard." He really liked and cared for Rick, like He did everyone. That night when Rick called, it was about 10 pm. Usually, he'd ask about work or the team. But this time, I told him that Cary's doctor said he wasn't going to make it. Rick asked me

"CARY SLOWLY STARTED REGAINING HIS STRENGTH. THE NEXT FEW YEARS WITH HIM WOULD BE THE BEST YEARS"

his symptoms and I described them the best I could with what was going on. Rick gave us hope when he said "I think I know what it is. Bring him up to the hospital and let me run some tests." Around 11 pm, the nurses ran a test where Cary drank some fluid and then we

"Cary with Franklin the day before his surgery. We thought he was gone."

watched from behind the screen what was happening to his passageways and stomach. It was just what Rick thought it was. He told us that doctors miss this all the time because they don't know what to look for.

Cary was literally starving to death. Because of the curvature of his spine, which was hard to look at, it was keeping food from getting to his stomach and being digested. His symptoms now made since. After putting Cary on IV's for the night, Rick reconstructed his stomach the next morning so that food could get through, actually two different passageways now, safely and without being hindered any longer. Rick was so confident, which quieted our nerves.

A couple of years later, when introducing Dr. Ranne as the doctor who gave me more time with Cary, he told me he wasn't sure if the procedure would work or not. Guess I'm glad he didn't inform me of that small detail before the surgery.

Cary slowly started regaining his strength. The next few years with him would be the best years, but not for the reasons someone might think. Because of a basketball relationship with Dr Ranne, God had given us a grace period that I will forever be grateful for. Dr. Ranne, thank you.

Always a smile!

CHAPTER 14

Dad, Am I Going to Die?

"And I will very gladly spend and be
spent for you."

2 Corinthians 12:15

*"If you spend yourself out physically, you become exhausted;
but spend yourself spiritually, and you get more strength.
God never gives strength for tomorrow, but only for
the strain of the minute."*

OSWALD CHAMBERS

(Baptist preacher and author)

It's hard to describe what kind of kid Cary was, but I need to try. He was extraordinary and an incredibly stubborn kid with a photographic mind.

Just about every night, I'd read the boys a book and then the Bible, or the Children's Bible for awhile. Cary would remember dates, and names and stories that I couldn't believe.

He would argue with me about some topic and never admit to being wrong. In the middle of the night, for years, he'd yell and I'd go running in to check on him. One time, both my legs were asleep and after jumping out of the bed,

I fell flat on my face. Of course, he laughed at me. We were always worried about him laying on his arm wrong or being uncomfortable someway. For years, I learned to sleep so light, that anything would wake me up. Sometimes when he'd yell for me, "Dad, Dad, Dad," I would go in the room and he'd want to argue about what we were talking about the evening before. He'd even wake up the next morning and want to argue some more. I was thankful for his toughness though, it made him strong-minded. He was much tougher than me. Cary didn't like for me to ask how he was doing. He'd say "Dad, don't ask." He didn't want anyone to feel sorry for him.

Oswald Chambers says "If we give way to self-pity and indulge in the luxury of misery, we banish God's riches from our own lives and hinder others from entering into His provision. No sin is worse than the sin of self-pity, because it obliterates God and puts self-interest upon the throne." Cary was helping teach me that having self-pity and being a victim served no purpose and actually cripples us in our daily walk with God. Being content, living with a thankful heart and having joy are impossible if we think of ourselves as victims and are drowning in self-pity.

For years, I read every animal book I could find for the boys. The week I read them *Summer of the Monkeys,* when the monkeys draped women's undergarments in the trees, Cary's stomach hurt and he couldn't talk because he would laugh so hard that there would be tears in his eyes. He would also make me turn the channel while watching good TV shows when they became embarrassing and he couldn't take it anymore.

I'd walk by his door and yell at him and he'd yell back "Hey weirdo." Other times, he'd just say "Love you, Dad!" I sure miss those times. He really meant it too.

Because he always hurt, when he felt the best and wanted to talk the most was about 11 pm or 12 am because his body would relax. He'd call me in to talk and we'd visit about everything, and he'd ask me questions or tell me what he'd been thinking about that day. Our conversations went from light and fun, to deep and serious. Every night, it would be a deep subject about life, or girls, or his relationship with God. Before the surgery, Cary would mention God, but I could never get much out of him, and his relationship with God concerned me. After the surgery, Cary would talk about God in profound ideas and thoughts and even his worship of God which not many young kids consider. To my great joy, I came to learn that Cary had a deep and very special relationship with Jesus Christ.

We would talk about Aaron and how he was concerned about him. He talked about honor a lot and how it made him sad that Aaron wasn't a person of honor, which to Cary meant you were a truth-teller and would do the right thing with integrity no matter what.

"IF WE GIVE WAY TO SELF-PITY AND INDULGE IN THE LUXURY OF MISERY, WE BANISH GOD'S RICHES FROM OUR OWN LIVES AND HINDER OTHERS FROM ENTERING INTO HIS PROVISION."

Cary was someone who guarded his mind and was careful what he thought or watched on TV. Because of his disease, he had a seriousness about life that wasn't normal for a kid his age. He also had a tenderness and empathy that is unusual as well. When someone in our extended family got pregnant before marriage, he told me it made him sad. Cary's desire was to be holy and honor God with his life.

Interestingly, he always had big dreams like robotic legs that could help him walk, or his ideas on science fiction and how he'd like to write a book someday.

> "BECAUSE OF HIS DISEASE, HE HAD A SERIOUSNESS ABOUT LIFE THAT WASN'T NORMAL FOR A KID HIS AGE."

One of his favorite experiences was when he got to visit with Spock and Captain Kirk because he loved Star Trek and futuristic ideas. The festival was on a Saturday. There were numerous booths that had all kinds of experiences and things to buy. Cary enjoyed everything, but he especially wanted to see Spock. Spock's quirky personality intrigued Cary. It's no surprise that his favorite shows were of characters that were a little bit different such as Alf, or Columbo the backwards detective that you would never know what he was going to ask or was thinking. Cary went from booth to booth looking for Spock until he finally showed up. He was very excited when he got his autograph on a Spock large figurine that I still have in a custom box. It was fun hearing him talk about how Spock

"Cary's with his favorite Aunt."

and Captain Kirk were good friends and they both liked to tease one another.

My sister Deana would drive every Saturday from Del City to Jenks, where we lived, to spend the day with Cary and my mom. Cary loved these two very much and had a special relationship with them. He loved to tease them and then would laugh so hard that he couldn't talk and tears would come to his eyes. Deana was like his big sister. The two of them would spoil Cary like crazy. They would take him and Franklin, his service dog, anywhere he wanted to go; restaurants, stores, movies and buy him whatever he asked for. It was their way of making his life special every week.

A friend from Church hooked us up with a special friend who happened to be a monkey. He would come over to the house about once every two weeks and sit on Cary's lap in the wheelchair and they would visit for a couple hours. The monkey loved to get candy from Cary's mouth and it became a game. He would pet Cary, groom him and they would share food. He would run through the house and we learned early on that you don't say no to him because he would bite me. I teased him with candy one time and he let me have it.

"Cary's monkey friend."

Never have I been bit by a snake, but it couldn't have hurt any worse.

Remarkably, Cary went from not being able to read, to reading novels in one year. Teachers didn't think he was very smart because he talked slow and was very thoughtful before he talked. He wanted to talk but you had to give him time to speak.

Finally, he ran into a teacher that expected everything out of him. Everything from "No Cary, you can't run over other kids with your wheelchair" to "read that book for me." Because she raised the bar with him, he started reading novels. He'd read a huge book and finish it quickly. Science fiction was his favorite. I'd ask him how it was and he'd say just ok. Even though he didn't like it much, he had to finish. He sure was a determined little kid. I still remember her having to unplug his wheelchair so he wouldn't run over kids when he got mad.

Cary loved the water because it was the one place he felt comfortable and couldn't hurt himself. Just like any kid, I'd throw him as high as I could and quickly grab him out of the water. In the later years, I got a lot more conservative but still had fun with him in the water.

Cary inherited my love for animals so we took every opportunity to provide different experiences for him.

We drove to Arkansas a couple of times to an animal reserve where we got to hold different baby animals and experience a lot of different species. One time I was teasing a monkey that was on the windshield and I wasn't giving him his food quick enough, so he jumped at me showing his teeth which scared the living daylights out of me, which of course the boys thought was hysterical. There was another animal rescue in Broken Arrow, Oklahoma and the manager, a really kind lady,

"My favorite animals."

stayed open after hours so Cary could have access by himself with all the animals. We loved these times because it meant so much to Cary.

When Cary got his Swedish wheelchair, we would have to chase him all over the zoo which gave him a lot of satisfaction. For once, he wasn't the slow handicapped kid. He'd ask me with a smartelec grin on his face if I was getting tired yet.

Cary didn't have a lot of friends, but the ones he did have meant the world to him. I would work hard to get people to come over to visit him so that he wouldn't be so lonely. He loved people visiting and would talk to them for the longest time, whether it was Dr. Ranne, our preacher Glenn Plum, or his youth pastor Kevin Laufer, or his best friend Robbie. He started having to wear oxygen so it became harder to get around. It was difficult to keep his spirits up but remarkably, he worked at keeping mine up instead. Everyday, it was "You doing ok dad?". He'd ask me questions and want to know how my day had been.

There was a lady friend who was a barber that started coming to the house to give him a haircut.

For some reason, all of my sisters and all the women and young ladies we were around loved to kiss Cary on the cheek. He would always shy away from it, but I really think he enjoyed the attention.

His favorite thing to do was draw. I signed him up for art camp a couple of times, but mostly, we'd buy him drawing books that he'd learn and draw from. Robotic looking stuff was probably his most favorite because he was a big fan of anything and everything Star Trek. Those were the days when there were a lot of cast off shows from Star Trek and he watched them all. Because of his youth pastor at Church and a couple of friends, he really started liking Christian music, which I was excited about. So, we bought him a boombox and a number of cassette tapes to listen to.

One year out of the blue, Cary decided he wanted to be called Matt instead of Cary. Matthew was his middle name so it wasn't an odd request, I guess. He informed everyone of the change and it was a big deal to him. One day the youth pastor from Church was over and was trying to talk to Cary, but he was ignoring him. Kevin couldn't figure out what was wrong. Finally, he recalled the name change and referred to him as Matt. Of course, Matt immediately started answering him. That's the stubbornness I talked about. By the way, I'm also stubborn and I refused to change, but he let me get away with it.

Cary meant, 'beloved' and his name meant too much for me to change. He was named after my cousin I grew up with who I'd still rather be with than any close friend.

Only the strong can help the weak: but who are the strong? Kevin would bring kids over who were struggling with their attitude, or home life or whatever, and would tell them that they are going over to encourage a young man with muscular dystrophy in a wheelchair. Instead, what Kevin was doing was using Cary to help change their lives by changing their perspective. Here was a kid who had every reason to complain in life but instead, he encouraged

ONLY THE STRONG CAN HELP THE WEAK: BUT WHO ARE THE STRONG?

others in life; always asking how they are doing and showing care and concern. He had a thankful, loving heart and young men would go away with a whole new outlook. Only the strong can help the weak.

Besides taking Cary to a Bulls game, my dad and I also got tickets to a Dallas Mavericks game. Denny Price got the tickets from Mark, his son, who played for the Cleveland Cavaliers who were coming into Dallas. Mark was great about visiting with the boys in the downstairs lounge before the game. We also tried a hockey game but it was a bad experience when the bathrooms weren't set up for his wheelchair and we had to leave abruptly.

Sadly though, soon after our trip to Dallas, Cary stopped liking sports and even basketball. He told me, "Dad, it's too hard to watch others play when I can't." Instead, I would take him to Christian concerts or movies. It became difficult, trying to find things he could enjoy and look forward to.

The Muscular Dystrophy Association helped tremendously. They supplied us with his hospital bed, his first two wheelchairs and other smaller items. He also got to attend the MDA summer camps which was by the way, hard to let him go. He attended the camp for three years and had the same really cute blonde, blue eyed young lady as his counselor. She was great to Cary and he needed her kindness and encouragement. They of course, would have a really hard time saying goodbye each time. Cary also got to attend camp Barnabus two years as he got older. God always knows what's best because this time, he needed a male role model and he gave Cary a perfect one. I'll always remember and be thankful for the sacrifice, love and concern these two young people gave Cary.

As everyone knows, the MDA has the big telethon every year. I'm not sure why, but I had an idea. The local TV station that was doing the telethon would always do a story on Cary either at our house or the zoo; some place he could be comfortable. He would come across as the sweetest, most adorable blonde, blue-eyed kid on the TV screen. They would capture his heart and spirit everytime. It didn't hurt that he had a precious smile as well. MDA told me that everytime his story would run every few hours, the phones would all light up.

In 2000 and 2001, Cary got so bad that we were able to get our insurance to pay for a hospital nurse to come in and care for Cary. She was a wonderful nurse and became a good friend and Cary loved her very much. He needed someone who was patient and kind hearted, and that was her. She loved him so much that when it was time for her to finish her nursing degree and

"Cary with his best friend ."

go back to school, she decided to wait so she could be with Cary. We will always be grateful to Melissa. She is now a full-time nurse at St. Francis in Tulsa, Ok.

All through Cary's life, God put special friends like Roby, his tall 6'-7" friend, who invited Cary to spend the night. Cary was hard to take care of, but the family took on the challenge. Friends like his youth pastor Kevin, the camp counselors, Dr Ranne, and Glenn, our pastor, who all cared for him greatly.

God also gave him a special gift, as Martha was a nurse and she took special care of him. She always knew what to do and prevented things like bed sores, chaffing, cramps, constipation, and all problems that kids with Muscular Dystrophy face. God of course, knew what he was doing because there were many times I was of no help because of my squeamish stomach.

One time, we were watching a TV show and a commercial came on about a kid dying. I remember Cary turning around at about the age of 9 or 10 asking and telling me "Dad, I'm not going to die, am I? I know I'm not, am I Dad?" Of course I lied. He would know soon enough.

A few years later, I remember talking to Cary about Heaven and running and having dogs and even though he didn't say it, I knew he had figured out he was going to die. He wasn't afraid though. Sometimes he would sound sad but he wouldn't stay there.

My name, Donald, means "overcomer". I was getting ready to face the biggest obstacle of my life and would need the power of God to overcome. Only the strong can help the weak.

Cary called Franklin his "buddy." He was his closest companion.

CHAPTER 15
"Dad, I'm really tired tonight." CARY
"MATTHEW" CALVERT
(1982-2002)

"In the world, ye shall have
tribulation: but be of good cheer;
I have overcome the world."

John 16:33

*"An average view of the Christian life is that it means deliverance
from trouble, which is very different."*

OSWALD CHAMBERS

(Baptist preacher and author)

The book of Esther is probably my favorite book in the Bible and I really love the story. We'd all like to think that our lives count and that it matters: that we are the one that will make the difference. Being born "for such a time as this," like in Esther, gives us meaning and purpose for each day.

The days were long and difficult in 2002. Martha was unhappy with me most of the time and Aaron was starting to share the same attitude such as mistrust, disrespect, blame for his bad attitude or for things that didn't go well, or that somehow I was a bad guy in all of this.

Cary was basically in pain and discomfort all of the time. He would apologize for me having to clean him up and that broke my heart. Franklin, his service dog, wouldn't leave his side because he knew Cary was hurting. He would lay on him every chance he got which would help comfort Cary and ease his pain.

It was a Friday and I got finished about 6pm or 7pm and went straight home. Saturdays for Score were always full and the schedule was always tricky trying to organize it. There was one lady in particular that wouldn't cooperate. She would always wait until the last minute to let me know whether her team was coming or not. If so, then I had to move everyone around to accommodate her, and if not, move everyone up. This particular night, it took me forever to get the schedule fixed for the next day, and so I didn't take the time to visit with Cary much that evening. By the time I went to visit him and talk for awhile, he told me "Dad, I'm really tired tonight." I told him I loved him and we'd talk more tomorrow. I kissed him on the forehead and said "Good night." I'm sure I watched TV for a couple of hours and then went to bed. It was going to be a long day of lessons tomorrow.

> **"EVEN THOUGH I KNEW HEAVEN WAS INCREDIBLY BETTER FOR HIM, MY HEART ACHED FOR A COUPLE OF YEARS FOR ONE MORE CONVERSATION AND ONE MORE HUG."**

I got up about 7:15 am and went into Cary's room to check on him. When I walked in, I could tell immediately that he was gone. I yelled out to Martha and then started sobbing and yelling, "No, God! No! Not my Cary!" Even now, my eyes fill up with tears and my forehead gets really tight with a headache and my chest hurts and it's been over 17 years since his death.

First thing I did was call my mom and then our pastor, Glenn. Everything after that was a blur. All I remember was the funeral home coming over and a couple of people dropping by. But mainly, I remember wanting to desperately hold him and hug him one more time. It was incredibly sad watching Franklin look lost, wondering what was going on. I loved kissing Cary on the cheek and hugged him and told him I loved him. Reality was a thousand pounds of bricks on my chest.

That was a Saturday morning, March 23rd, 2002. Cary was 5' 7", 50 lbs when he passed away. It was a miserable life he was living, but I still wanted one more day with him. Cary knew he was going to die and I tried to get ready. Even though I knew Heaven was incredibly better for him, my heart ached for a couple of years for one more conversation and one more hug. I've tried to tell myself that the last night doesn't matter, that there were lots of meaningful conversations the last few weeks, but my heart still ached with regret and pain for not spending that last night with him the whole evening. Really, I'm not sure it would ease the pain even for a second, but I still beat myself up for a long time after that. As so many know, the pain of regret is very powerful.

We already had a grave site I had purchased four years earlier when we didn't know if Cary was going to make it or not. I went by myself and picked out his grave stone. It read Cary Matthew Calvert and had a Star Trek Voyager on it, a dog that looked like Franklin and the word "Beloved" on it.

At his funeral, the Church was packed. Many of my teacher friends, Sr Mary Clare and of course, Pete Theban, were there from Monte Cassino. Afterwards, Pete gave me an envelope with cash that everyone at Monte Cassino had collected to help with the funeral. Their sacrifice brought warmth to my soul and meant a lot.

"Cary and his bear."

Lots of former students and parents, as well as Church friends showed up and paid their respects. I enjoyed seeing everyone there, especially all of my family and relatives. Having a close family helped tremendously, but I wished that I could comfort Martha and Aaron more. All I could do was pray. I knew they were hurting as much as I was.

Talking to my good friend, John Hewitt, who along with Bill Coppoc was always a source of strength and peace. I asked John if he would sing at Cary's funeral and he agreed. He played his guitar and sang "I Can Only Imagine" by Mercy Me. The song, to this day, puts a lump in my throat but has a special message of hope. It is no coincidence that the movie about the song and Mercy Me came out at the same time I am writing this book.

The youth pastor, Kevin, spoke and we all laughed with him as he told "Cary" stories and felt proud when he described his character. My sister, Deana, spoke next. I had chosen her to write his eulogy for the paper and she further expanded on her thoughts about Cary. It was only by God's grace that she made it through. She read the paper slow and with an understanding of Cary that only she could convey to everyone there. I wanted everyone there to know the Cary that I knew and just how incredible his life was.

Just like Esther, his life had meaning and purpose. I prayed for years that Cary would be healed and many people prayed for him to be as well. We had a special time of prayer with many people and I had the faith in God for him to be released but I won't find out until Heaven the "whys" for everything. Until then, my memories will have to do. Here's the beautiful words Deana spoke that day:

> "There is no possible way I could put into words what Cary meant to me. He kept life in perspective for me. He loved my Brett. He taught me far too much because there is just simply no one like my Cary Matthew. Yes, there were years of frustration, heartaches and pain that I will never forget. He shaped our family and made us stay before God in prayer. But when I close my eyes, what I will see is blonde hair (but no blonde jokes please), laughter, and man, he said the funniest things in all the world. I will remember video games and sci-fi and all the adventures we went on together. My heart will melt when I hear him say, "How are you doing Deana?" or "Grandma, Grandma" a thousand times. I will remember the incredible talks that took place between father and son that most will never comprehend

and how only Mom could make him comfortable and give him peace so much of the time. "Mom are you there?" I will miss his thousand questions and insights, his orneriness, amazing courage and complete love. Best of all, I will hear "I love you Franklin" and feel blow kisses and see his wonderful hands. Cary always used to say he wanted to be a hero. To all of us, he simply was. Thank you so much for giving him to us."

- DEANA WEBBER

A couple of weeks before Cary died, we talked about Heaven and with my help, Cary planned out his funeral. It included seven things, or wishes. He didn't know how hard it was to discuss these things. He was much stronger than me. The list read like this:

- » Cary doesn't want anyone to cry at his funeral

- » Wants me to keep getting the Sigel comics (his favorite)

- » He wants there to be a party at his funeral

- » Mark will sing (our music director who he liked a lot)

- » Tell people about Jesus so Robbie can go to Heaven (his best friend)

- » Wants Robbie to read the whole Bible (NIV)

- » Coffin shaped like a spaceship

I knew Cary was bad, but you just hope somehow the days won't end. While trying to help give meaning to Cary's life and everyone's involvement with him, I wrote these words and was going to read them at the funeral, but when the time came, it was too painful.

No one has ever seen or heard what I wrote. It went like this: Matt was someone who needed lots of care and attention. The last couple of years, he reached the point where, because of his limitations, he led a very limited and lonely life. Things would have been unbearable except for his relationships.

Robbie, Matt always thought of you as his best friend. You stayed with him through everything. He loved talking to you and would tell everyone how tall you are.

Melissa, you and Franklin were his most trusted companions. He loved you dearly and so does our entire family because of what you gave to his life. You made life bearable for Cary, Aaron, Martha and myself. There's no way to thank you enough.

Deana, you gave meaning and joy to his life. He looked forward to his weekends because of you. Your sacrifice made it easier for me to be away from him on a long day. He loved asking you a million questions and teasing you and Mom.

Mom, he counted on you like we did. I'm so thankful he got to spend these couple of years with you. Some of my fondest memories are of Cary and how he loved to tease Deana and you. You drew him closer to God every time he was around you.

Aaron, you were a great brother to Cary. Thanks for being good to him even when it was difficult. He told me a couple of weeks ago that he loved you. Your mom and my greatest joy came when we'd hear you and him talking in his room.

Martha, no mother ever sacrificed more than you. You're the only one that could comfort him and the only one that would do when he was hurting the most. You're the reason he lived four more good years. When push came to shove, only you would do.

Cary loved these and many others as only he could, including Kevin, Mark, Ben, Dr. Ranne, Glenn and many others. His relationships were his life. Over the last couple of years my greatest prayer for him came true with the development of his most important relationship however, and that was his friendship and love for Jesus Christ. God graciously blessed him with the gift of himself and that's how Cary made it. When I would come home late at night, I'd barely be in the door and Cary would be yelling, "DAD!" He would be ready for me to read the Bible to him. Cary knew that Jesus Christ is the one that would make a difference in his life. When Matt was planning his funeral a couple of weeks ago, he was at peace because of his relationship with Jesus. He knew that Jesus loved him and died for him so that he could be in Heaven one day.

There were so many things he looked forward to here on earth like, writing a book, going to college, and he really wanted to get married, but he knew Heaven was his permanent home. If you think that was easy for him, you don't understand his pain and suffering. If ever someone felt sins affect on his body, it was Cary. If you understand that, only then can you begin to understand how much Jesus loved Cary and Cary Matthew knew it.

His greatest desire when he was planning his funeral for three days was his desire that some would hear the gospel about God's great love shown to us on the cross and that you could have the same relationship that he had with Jesus. He knew that Jesus' Friendship had made the difference.

Cary's grave with the beautiful flowers. Love it being under a beautiful tree also.

25 year anniversary of our winning the Big 8 at O.U. in 1979.
(L to R) Myself, Ray Whitley, Carry Carrabine, "Pugs" Our Manager, and Aaron Curry.

CHAPTER 16

The World Stops for No One
(Calm in the Storm)

"But let patience have her perfect
work, that ye may be perfect and
entire, wanting nothing."

James 1:4

*"If we keep true to God, God will take us through an ordeal which
will bring us out into a better knowledge of Himself."*

OSWALD CHAMBERS

(Baptist preacher and author)

Glenn, my pastor, used to tell me that scars were a sign of injury, but they were also a sign of healing. I took a couple of weeks off and then went back to training. The kids were the only ones that kept my mind off of Cary. Fortunately, Therapeutics let us keep Franklin and he would go to the gym everyday with me, which he loved. I still remember having to go find him in another gym while he was enjoying a birthday party. The lights were out and he was laying by a bunch of kids, sharing their popcorn. He was on a strict diet unless we were at the movies with Cary and he'd eat the popcorn off the ground.

Franklin started going to a nursing home as a therapy dog and he was great with everyone there, and they of course loved him. Franklin concerned me because he had taken care of Cary for years and now he didn't have his buddy anymore, which is what Cary called him. The nursing home and gym helped him not to be depressed but he would still be looking around for Cary. I may have been imagining him looking lost, but I don't think so.

In God's grace, He knew how much Franklin would encourage me. Every good and perfect gift is from above and Franklin was perfect for me. He knew over 70 commands but it always cracked me up that a Labrador didn't like the water. He would hide under the bed when it was bath time and I'd have to drag him out, and he didn't like retrieving either. I'd throw the ball for him and he'd look at me like "Why would I want to go run after that?".

> **"GOD, ONCE AGAIN, GAVE ME THE GRACE TO NOT ANSWER HER IN ANGER, BUT TO JUST LISTEN AND PRAY."**

Remember that God had promised me before I got married that no disease would overtake me. I wasn't so sure. That summer, I was trying hard to move on and make the most out of life. First thing I did was build a deck for the back porch for Martha. My dad helped me and it turned out great. Next, I bought a storage building and put it in the backyard so we could organize things better.

Dad and I also took out our carpet and put in ceramic tile which made our house look a lot better. The carpet had taken a beating with the wheelchair over the years.

Martha and I then went on a trip to Branson for a couple of days and left Aaron by himself with his promise that he'd have no one over. We had an okay time, but things were pretty cold. What I didn't know was Martha was telling different friends of hers that she was going to divorce me after Cary died. A couple of nights before we were supposed to come home, I got a call from the police saying that my son was having a huge party at the house and the police had been called by neighbors. Needless to say, I was very disappointed and angry at Aaron. We left Branson the next morning and headed home. On the way, Martha let me have it and blamed me for everything. She used every device she could think of to hurt me, even telling me that I couldn't even spend time with my son the night before he died. God, once again, gave me the grace to not answer her in anger, but to just listen and pray. Don't get me wrong, I wanted to let her have it, but I was able to show her grace instead and kept quiet.

We cleaned up the mess when we got home. Over the next few weeks, Martha was very hostile and kept threatening to divorce me. I knew she was hurting like me, but there wasn't anything I could say to ease the pain.

Glenn, my pastor, and I spent time together and he let me know that God would answer my prayer for our marriage in one of three ways. He would change Martha's heart and we'd have a good marriage, or God would allow her heart to turn cold and she'd divorce me, or she'd stay the same and God would give me the grace to love her even if she chose not to love me. Of course I wanted the first choice, but would settle for the second one. Surely the third one wasn't an option I wanted. My prayer though was that God's will be done and that He would be glorified. It was my responsibility to do the right thing whether I was being treated right or not.

Martha kept threatening me and I finally decided to talk to her to settle things once and for all. My heart really was to love Martha and build a life with her. We had already made it through the tough times and why not go make the most of things now, or so I thought.

My conversation with Martha went something like this; "Martha, I love you very much and I want to be married to you for the rest of my life. However, I don't want you threatening me anymore. Either divorce me or let's get on with our lives and make the most of things." This was a Monday or Tuesday, and by Friday, she served me divorce papers at the gym. When I got home after work that Friday, she had changed the locks and put all of my clothes and other stuff on the front porch in garbage bags.

That night, I called a friend who let me stay in his bus that was like a mobile home on wheels. We parked it behind Champions and Franklin and I stayed there for a few months. Getting an apartment or moving in with my parents didn't sound good. Legally, I could have moved back into the house and make it a battle, but I just wanted to move out and start over. Living in the bus, I got very lonely and I was fighting depression all the time.

Aaron was staying with Martha but we were keeping in touch. He helped me get some more of my stuff out of the house but I didn't try to take advantage. One thing I learned from losing a child is that the world stops for no one. I wanted people to slow down and grieve with me and acknowledge that something horrible has happened and life is tragic and not the same.

I didn't want to move on in some ways because that meant Cary was no longer part of my life. In life though I learned, there are still bills to pay and work to be done and conversations to be had. While sitting in Church one day I was totally numb and knowing that no one knew how much I was hurting, I wrote these words on the Church program:

"Things are very difficult these days. My emotions go from sadness and anger, to despair and confusion. My spirit has given way to despair because of the hopelessness I feel inside. The numbness of my soul is only replaced by concern or worry of daily duties that must be done.

No more do prayers come easily or with feeling and emotion. There is no more excitement or looking forward; just

"I JUST WANTED TO MOVE OUT AND START OVER."

a dread for what is inevitable. I stay up late at night, not wanting to go to bed because when morning comes reality hits like a wave from the ocean. I always do my crying late at night. The dark cloud of reality hangs over my head continually. I've lost my breath—gasping as if someone has punched me in the stomach. Depression has hit me hard and I'm reeling from it's powerful blows. Like David in the Bible: "O that I had wings like a dove: I would fly away and be at rest. Yes, I would wander far away, I would lodge in the wilderness. I would hasten to escape and to find me a shelter from the stormy wind and tempest."

God as always gave me a promise in 2 Chronicles 15:7 that I would count on. "But as for you, be strong and do not give up, for your work will be rewarded." The message was always to stay faithful and God would bless me. What was important to me at this point was what David Wilkerson wrote in a letter that I received that said: "In the most trying of times, the Lord instructs us to rejoice and be glad in Him. In Psalm 9, David says, "I will be glad and rejoice in thee" (verse 2). Why? Because "the Lord also will be a refuge for the oppressed in times of trouble." (verse 9) I believe, that one of the greatest testimonies to a fearful and bewildered society will be the peace, joy and serenity of God's people in times of distress and terror. Those who trust the Lord completely will be given supernatural rest and peace.

Cary sitting in a fighter jet of the Blue Angels.

No evil report will rob them of their gift of confidence in God's faithfulness to them."

Then quietly, I'd remember good times with Cary and he'd bring a smile to my face. I'd remember the long talks and the meaningful conversations. I could see him looking at a pretty girl and not wanting me to tease him about her. He'd laugh so hard at times that he couldn't talk and I'd remember better times. I'll most remember holding his broken body in my arms and making things okay for a short time. He would look at me with those eyes and say "You doing okay Dad? Love you Dad."

Coaching the Saint Francis Hawks was a great distraction from every day struggles. (201-18)

CHAPTER 17

Off To Germany We Go!

"Strengthen ye the weak hands, and confirm the feeble knees. Say to them that are of a fearful heart, Be strong, fear not."

Isaiah 35:3,4

"The weaker and feebler you are, the better. The one who has something to trust in is the last one to come anywhere near saying, "I will serve the Lord."

OSWALD CHAMBERS

(Baptist preacher and author)

The divorce went through that winter and I was ready to turn the page. The night before the hearing, God was very encouraging to me. He told me: "Though you have made me see troubles, many and bitter, you will restore my life again; from the depths of the earth. You will again bring me up. You will increase my honor and comfort me once again." Psalm 71:20-21.

The divorce settlement couldn't have worked out any better. I was so glad to be through all of this. A friend of mine who was a pastor, was also a con artist, which I didn't know at the time, stole $36,000 from me which was basically all I had. He also stole $11,000 from my sister. Being a master deceiver, he took advantage of me at my weakest point. In deciding whether to take him to court and prove his deception, God gave me two promises. One was that he would take care of the man, (Deuteronomy 32:35 and Romans 12:19) and that he would bring one down and exalt another. The second promise was that He would restore everything.

So in great peace and confidence, I left everything to God. A couple of years after this, the man who stole all of the money died in a small plane crash. He was the pilot and ran out of gas. Other people can decide if this was God's doing or how it all fits. I don't need or want to be the judge. I definitely have my own struggles and sin to overcome. Just about everything had been taken away now; my home, wife, kids and money. To say this would be the end and things would become great after this, or even normal wouldn't be accurate, I would find out pretty soon.

Aaron was starting to do well and for the first time in a long time, was really working at making his life better. He was playing on my AAU basketball team, which was really good and he had played well all summer. For the first time, he was looking forward to school and the basketball team at school. Every child that goes through tragedy like losing their brother, or divorce, needs lots of help to work through grief and pain. He had quit self-medicating and started to clean himself up.

When school started, I was looking forward to Aaron having a good year and for things to get better, at least on one front. During tryouts, the head coach at Bixby High School called Aaron into his office and told him that he didn't want to mess with him this year and that he wouldn't be on the team. The "road to recovery" was side-tracked by a coach that chose not to invest in a grieving players life. Aaron wasn't easy to coach the year before, but I'm not sure how a 16 year old can handle the death of his brother or his parents divorcing any better. It wasn't because Aaron wasn't a good player, he should have started that year. He played well all summer with a really good attitude. I've heard the saying that "intolerant people have never suffered."

My disappointment in a coach that wouldn't try to help a hurting player was enormous. A coach from a local high school, Coach Scott, asked me how Aaron was doing a couple of weeks later. I told him what happened and what was said and his response was that "I wouldn't have one player on my team if I didn't help players like Aaron." After that, I found this song Aaron wrote that expressed how low he was feeling. Please excuse the language:

Smokin trees to fulfill my needs, Everyday
is the same, I just sit and gaze.

Cause I know s#@t will never change, things
still seem to remain the same and

I guess I'm to blame. But s#@t I get so sad that I don't know
what to do and I want to break down and cry, why the f@#k did
my brother die. I find myself askin why, but that ain't the half.

I don't know how much I got left. I'm too stressed. I don't even
want to go to school. I'm so screwed. I got f@#ked over and now

I have no money and no job and f...in parents got separated that
left me even more frustrated how much more s#@t can't even face
I'm about to break.

As always, I was trusting that God was sovereign and that everything works together for good to those who love God and are called according to His purposes. Of course, I wanted to be mad at the coach but it was time to trust God again. He was the one in control and not me. I firmly believed Hebrews 11:6 "And without faith it is impossible to please God, because anyone who comes to him must believe that he exists and that he rewards those who earnestly seek him."

It would take another book for me to explain what took place next, but needless to say, God works in mysterious ways. The short version is: There was a Church at Champions I started attending. A family at the Church that used to go to my other Church in Jenks was also attending. The husband, I would find out later was verbally abusive and was cheating on his wife. He was also divorcing her

"WE WERE MARRIED IN AUGUST OF 2003 IN EUREKA SPRINGS, ARKANSAS WITH ONLY A FEW RELATIVES PRESENT WHICH WAS HOW WE WANTED IT."

and running away with another woman. He also happened to be the man that stole the $36,000 from me. Furthermore, he led Bible studies at the Church and preached sometimes and was currently the new manager at Champions. It was quite a soap opera. I've always led a boring life and this was too much drama for me.

The interesting thing was that when I was in Jenks going to Church with my family; Karen, the wife, had started a ministry for our family where she would come over and take care of our son, bring him dinner and read with him, watch movies or whatever he wanted to do so Martha could have time off to get things done.

It's amazing how God puts things together because I didn't know Karen and she always came by while I was still at work. My divorce was final and so was hers in Late 2002. We didn't really date, we just kind of hung out together and we both really enjoyed one another's company. It didn't hurt that she loved the Lord, was hard-working, enjoyed animals and the outdoors, and of course was really "hot" as one of my AAU players called her when she came to a practice.

We were married in August of 2003 in Eureka Springs, Arkansas with only a few relatives present which was how we wanted it. Over the next few years, a lot of healing needed to take place, and God would need to work in both our lives. Our marriage was really good at times, but as expected, there were a lot of things to work on as well. What I didn't know was there were even more difficult trials coming and we needed each other. Karen was the perfect wife for what we were facing. She was tough, smart and fearless. She would encourage me in faith when I needed a literal push.

In 2006, my back started bothering me; back spasms, aching and nerve pain and we started trying everything to relieve the pain. We tried all kinds of supplements, chiropractor, some needling thing, stretching apparatus, inversion hanging machine, and of course, this interesting box thing from Arizona. Unfortunately, none of it worked. Every night I'd use ice packs to give me some relief, but it was only temporary.

By 2007, I'd had enough. The pain was making life unbearable and I wouldn't take pain pills because I didn't want to head down the road of addiction and dependence. We tried neurontin and lyrica but both of those made me feel loopy and like I had the flu. That was as bad as the nerve pain. I started spending most of my time in a wheelchair for about a year. We also tried tinge units and numerous spinal shots, but of course, none of it made a difference. The only thing that did help was a bowl of ice cream at night. My stomach was upset from the pain and the sugar would settle my stomach. After work I'd go lay down and Karen would bring me an ice pack and a bowl of ice cream. The only side effect was the 37 pounds I gained because I couldn't work out and get exercise. Reluctantly, we then started the long progression of back doctors or orthopedic surgeons. The first appointment was to a Doctor Hawkins, whose son I had trained a few years earlier. He recommended we try a surgery called a discectomy which didn't work for me and the tremendous pain continued unfortunately.

The next thing we did was get another MRI which was an adventure because after Cary died, I developed claustrophobia. I didn't know it until the technician put me in the machine and I had a panic attack. The lady wanted to suspend the MRI but I told her to give me a couple of minutes. She said no one had ever gone back in.

I made it through by concentrating on other things and praying and singing praise songs to myself. I made it through.

What Dr. Hawkins found this time was that I had four ruptured discs and was basically in trouble. Karen and I met with Dr. Hawkins to discuss our options. Best I can remember, because I was in shock when I heard four ruptured discs, three fusions and a couple of other things. He went on to tell us that I would need multiple surgeries and the discs above and below would go bad eventually, and that they weren't sure how much of the pain it would help with anyway. Lastly, I would more than likely end up in a wheelchair someday.

As we got ready to leave, (by now I was sick to my stomach) he took all the hardware that was proposed to go in my back and put it in Karen's hands. We looked at it for a second and then she handed it back. Next thing I know, we are walking out the door and Karen says to me so no one else could hear, "We aren't going to do this, are we?" I said of course not.

We talked on the way home of how God had promised to restore everything and I knew God didn't mislead me, so we knew this wasn't the plan. Again I was reminded; Why art thou dis-quieted within me oh my soul, hope thou in God. As always, I began to pray. In the meantime, I hired a former Arkansas player who came recommended to help coach because for the last few months, I had been teaching from a rolling office chair while only standing up or demonstrating when I had to. Other times, I was in a wheelchair that Karen would push me around in. Since I was coaching an AAU team again, parents and players would also help Karen push me around, especially when we traveled. The year 2007 was spent mostly in a wheelchair.

If this wasn't bad enough, the owners of Champions had decided to close because the land became worth more than the business. Now I was without a gym. We moved into the Jewish Center temporarily during this time, knowing it wouldn't work for a permanent place. Business for the first time was dwindling and things couldn't have been any worse.

"RIGHT BEFORE WE TOOK OFF, A STEWARDESS CAME TO US AND SAID THEY HAD 2 FIRST CLASS SEATS.".

The back problems and surgeries were put on hold until God provided the answer to an impossible situation. To be honest, I'd been through so much of this kind of struggle that I was determined as ever to trust God's plan.

One day I was talking to a friend of mine named Ted Davis whose daughters I had trained, conveying to him what I was up against. He told me about a friend who had the same back issues, multiple blown discs. The friend called me on a Friday evening and we talked for over an hour. There was a surgery in Germany that he was looking into called ADR's or artificial disc replacement. Needless to say, we were very interested. Karen is the research person; thankfully she loves to delve in deep.

That night, I went to bed on time while Karen stayed up reading late into the night. I woke up late because I tossed and turned all night before finally falling asleep. As soon as Karen saw the light come on, she ran into the bedroom and started jumping up and down yelling "We found it, this is it!" She had stayed up most of the night reading about Stenum Hospital in Bremen Germany where they do ADR surgeries.

A couple of doctors told us that Germany was 20 years ahead of us in back surgeries, just like they were in lasek eye surgery. I had one doctor tell me not to go because what happens if things don't go well. He was also a close friend that I relied on. The week before we left, he called me and reassured me that I was doing the right thing and God would be with me. Another doctor at Tulsa Bone and Joint, who I used to help me understand my x-rays, CT Scan and MRI's, when I asked him if Germany was the right move, he closed his door and then spoke quietly saying this was where I needed to go. There was an experimental ADR being done in Dallas I found out, but they were only doing one level, and they were having trouble with the procedure while using a disc that was obsolete in Germany. Needless to say, we were headed to Bremen Germany.

My pain level averaged an 8-10. The only thing that helped was eating and icing my back. The pain gave me nerve headaches, dizziness and nausea. This was what I was up against as we headed out.

We couldn't afford first class, but my wife approached the ticket counter and explained the situation while I prayed. The hardest thing for me to do was sit.

It would give me back spasms and intense nerve pain.

The airline personnel were very courteous but said it's against their policy and they didn't have room anyway and they were very sorry.

In December of 2007, we boarded the plane and sat down for what was going to be an excruciating plane ride. Right before we took off, a stewardess came to us and said they had two first class seats. Instead of a miserable trip, laying down most of the flight made it bearable and somewhat comfortable. I'm never surprised when God takes care of me, but I'm still amazed at His incredible kindness and mercy towards me.

When we got there, the hospital staff took x-rays and other tests. We later met with the head surgeon and his assistant to go over the results and discuss tomorrow's schedule. What they found wasn't good. In the month since the last MRI, my back was now collapsing and twisted. The doctors couldn't do the four ADR's that had been agreed upon by the email when they read my last MRI, but they could do a flexible fusion, and the rest of the ADR's which they confidently said would take care of my pain.

The x-rays made my heart sink and made me a little nauseated but it was time to trust God again and not to fear. About the time I get comfortable, God throws the impossible at me. In John 11:40 it says, "said I not unto thee, that, if thou wouldest believe, thou shouldest see the glory of God?"

The surgery couldn't have gone any better. The only bad part was that I had a terrible reaction to morphine and broke out all over. That was the most painful and uncomfortable 24 hours of my life with the itching, but there wasn't much they could do. We loved the doctors and nurses. The head nurse was a gentleman who had been with the hospital a long time and was also a Baptist preacher. No wonder I liked him so much.

One important side note was that Karen and I had to come up with the money ourselves because our insurance company kept giving us the runaround and we couldn't wait any longer. The cool part was, we had just enough money to pay for the surgery that we had been saving for a few years. At Stenum Hospital, whether you stay in the hospital

"The procedure was two ADR and one flexible fusion. To this day, you can still hear my back creaking from the flexible fusion."

one day or two weeks, it's the same cost. Karen was great because she didn't regret us spending all of our money one bit. The support and encouragement from Karen helped ease the difficulty.

The doctors cut me open in front and behind and kept me in the hospital for two weeks. The ADR is an interesting and brilliant procedure because they take out the damaged disc and replace it with a titanium disc that's like a ball and socket that is literally hammered into the bone of the spinal column. For a few weeks, I had to be careful not to move or twist quickly, so the disc could adhere to the bone.

After the two weeks in the hospital, we stayed at a really nice hotel in Bremen for a week to finish the rehab I would need before heading home. Karen and I fell in love with Germany and the German people. We loved the Christmas square, their love for the Bremen Soccer team, or football as they call it, and their German chocolate, bread, and ice cream. Karen would bring me meals from the restaurant down the street that was really nice. The hospital was out in the middle of nowhere. It was a beautiful countryside with farms all around. One of the rehab nurses took Karen to her farm one day so she could see all the horses and animals.

There was also a nice small family-owned hotel next door who didn't worry about payment or anything. They just made it as accommodating as possible, and you would pay when it was convenient. One of my young lady doctors that checked on me everyday was a huge soccer fan and would go to the matches all painted up with the other 40,000 people there. In Germany, young people were expected to do an internship for two years as a volunteer, so we had plenty of help pushing my wheelchair or retrieving things. Karen needed to go purchase some things the first week, so she rented a bicycle and rode into town which was quite a few kilometers away.

My hospital stay included rehab appointments and massage therapy as well. My massage therapist was a big

German who loved boxing. We spent a lot of time discussing Muhammad Ali and other great boxers. He wouldn't go to the soccer matches because he said the skinheads ruined it for everyone. They were too crazy he thought. Karen paid him extra money so that he'd come by everyday and even made a trip to the hotel in town to take care of me the next week. We paid him of course, but we both also had a lot of fun discussing sports. His pride and joy was his 1940 or 1950-something Mercedes convertible that was still in pristine shape.

One night at the hotel, we were in the square where the Christmas festival was taking place. There was a soccer match that night and everyone was dressed up and drinking beer outside watching the numerous TV's and yelling and having lots of fun. My favorite thing at the square was the bratwurst hot dogs and every other kind of hot dog you could think of.

> **"MY MASSAGE THERAPIST WAS A BIG GERMAN WHO LOVED BOXING. WE SPENT A LOT OF TIME DISCUSSING MUHAMMAD ALI AND OTHER GREAT BOXERS."**

Every day and night at the hospital, I couldn't understand the TV but Karen had purchased a portable DVD player so that I could watch episodes of *Mash* or Barney and Andy on Mayberry. I had enough DVD's to last the 3 weeks of old TV shows from the 70's and 80's I hadn't watched in years but enjoyed. It beat watching curling or dart throwing on TV.

My roommate was a guy from Kentucky who was a former football coach. One night, we watched the Dallas Cowboys beat someone at 3 am or so on his computer.

He came by himself but was fortunate because Karen helped take care of him which he appreciated.

The food for a hospital was great because they'd bring German bread and fruit and some things that were okay. After the first week, they had one of the interns wheel me downhill to Karen's hotel so we could spend a couple hours together. German hospitals and surgeries are done differently. They don't use antibiotics and they don't have trouble with infections or sickness because the rooms are all independently heated and cooled. Everyday, whether it's 70 degrees or 20 degrees outside, they open the windows for 30 minutes to clear out the air and freshen things up. To keep from freezing, you just wrap up in the blankets.

Bremen hospital is a beautiful place and was used as a barracks for the Germans in World War II interestingly enough. One of the last nights there, a cab picked us up and we were taken to a Mexican restaurant not far from the hospital. The food was great and it was good to get out if only for a couple of hours.

At the small restaurant, there was also a banquet hall and on Friday night, there was a band that would play music all evening and people would come from all over the countryside to join in. The place was packed and they had so much fun. Not sure if it was polka music, but I know it wasn't hip hop. I wish I could have joined in for the food and fun.

The way Germans go for walks every evening with their dogs or ride bicycles everywhere, or the way they sat around after dinner and would talk for an hour or so really appealed to us. God's favor was on us the entire trip and we were blessed beyond belief. All this became very important in a few years as God would open doors and give me a desire I never thought I'd have.

Bear, my new score mascot.

CHAPTER 18
God's Standards Are Higher Than Our Own

"But as he which hath called you is holy, so be ye holy in all manner of conversation."

1 Peter 1:15

"Never tolerate through sympathy with yourself or with others any practice that is not in keeping with a holy God."

OSWALD CHAMBERS

(Baptist preacher and author)

We all have standards, what we will settle for in life. The measure of a man can be easily defined by what he will allow himself to do or think on a consistent basis. A man is no better than his daily habits and his daily thought processes.

One of the things God did in my life was to raise the bar. He started setting the standard higher and higher for me. I believed in faith but was I a man of faith? Yes I prayed but was I a man of prayer? Did I base my life on prayer and faith? I was supposed to love others but was love the standard with which I lived my life. How was I going to allow myself to think or act on a consistent basis. I had every reason to blame others, or to feel sorry for myself, but that's not the standard God set before me. He didn't force me to live a life pleasing to Him. He just put the standard out there and said; "If you want to be my follower then you will spend time in prayer everyday, you will forgive others no matter what they do or say, you will be thankful and praise me and you will live by faith and wait on me." Defining a Christian life as on fire or lukewarm was too simplistic though because I was working non-stop, battling health and financial issues and trying to make a family work, etc. But somehow God slowed things down and started clearly defining the standard as one where the follower is broken before Him, dependent upon him and seeking Him. "Seek ye first the kingdom of God and all these things will be added unto you" was the measure of my day and the faith, obedience and love which was practiced, was the standard to live by and would define whether I was successful or not.

"GOD HAS A TENDERNESS TOWARDS ME THAT I CAN'T REALLY EXPLAIN ADEQUATELY. IT'S SOMETHING I WOULDN'T TRADE FOR ANY RICHES OR LIFESTYLE."

In the movie *Count of Monte Cristo*, the count, Jim Caviezel, wants justice and passionately wanted to destroy the men who stole much of his life and put him in prison. After realizing just how fortunate he had become and all that he had to live for, he changed the standard of his life to instead give grace and in turn, found peace and joy. What was used for evil towards him, would be the very means whereby he would gain wisdom, strength and friendship; not to mention great wealth. He no longer wanted to gain revenge, instead, he wanted to use his life for good, give grace, and demonstrate love.

A lot of us want to be inspired by great blessings, an inspiring word from God or entertaining Christian music that will move us to go on and be the kind of person that God will bless greatly. For us to go on with God, we need inspiration, we think, but "what hinders me from hearing God is that I am taken up with other things. If I am devoted to things, to service, to convictions, God may say what He likes but I do not hear Him. Narrow all your interests until the attitude of mind and heart and body is concentration on Jesus Christ." For me, the standard became about the relationship I have with Christ each day. The success of my day was and is now measured by my quality time with Him. I learned that prayer doesn't prepare me for the battle, but instead, it was the battle. I was only as good, or affective, as I enabled Him to live through me. This was dependant on the amount of time spent with Him, allowing Him to be my heavenly father, and Lord, and take over every aspect of my life.

God has a tenderness towards me that I can't really explain adequately. It's something I wouldn't trade for any riches or lifestyle. Something happened in my heartache and loneliness. God became my 'Abba" Father, my Prince of Peace who knew me before I was born, or as the Bible says in Psalm 139:17-18 "How precious to me are your thoughts, O God! How vast is the sum of them!

Were I to count them, they would outnumber the grains of sand. When I awake, I am still with you.".

Now, the standard was to maintain that relationship at all costs. Seems like a simplistic way of living, but everything emanates from that standard. All decisions and actions are now made from that standard.

Taking a walk with my horse, Bently.

CHAPTER 19

The Road to Restoration

"But they that wait upon the Lord
shall renew their strength; they shall
mount up with wings as eagles."

Isaiah 40:31

*"The surf that distresses the ordinary swimmer produces in the
surf-rider the super-joy of going clean through it."*

OSWALD CHAMBERS

(Baptist preacher and author)

The surgery went well and now it was time for the rehab.
I had to basically retrain myself to walk and move correctly,
or normal again, and start using muscles I had not used in a
long time. It seemed impossible but I had a terrific trainer
named Terry Lade that got me back in sound physical shape
and from there it was up to me to be disciplined to do my
work everyday.

Karen and I knew we couldn't stay at the Jewish Center
and our business survive, so we started looking for a
permanent solution. There was a warehouse complex that
we had driven by at least 100 times on Memorial in Bixby,
not too far from where Champions was and where we lived.

The roof, I was sure, was way too low for basketball training. To Karen's credit, she suggested we at least take a look. There was an empty warehouse that we found open that wasn't quite finished. First thing I did was start measuring to see if it was wide and long enough. Next, I got my dad and a friend to help me figure out if it was tall enough. My dad held a 10 foot board up like a basketball goal while I simulated what a shot from 20 feet would look like since the high school and college three point line was under 21 feet. Best we could tell, the roof was tall enough.

"ONE OF MY FORMER STUDENTS AND PLAYERS ON MY AAU TEAMS, MARCUS HALL TOOK CARE OF US AS A SALESMAN. THAT BEGAN A 10 YEAR RUN OF GREAT FUN AND SUCCESS WITH MARCUS AS MY SECOND COACH."

Next, I called the owner, TJ Remy to ask him if the lights, air conditioning , heating, and electrical pipes could all be raised up and the steel posts in the middle removed. At first, he said yes on everything except the posts. When I told him that it wasn't possible then, he called the builder to see what could be done. Thankfully, the builder informed TJ that they were just extra support and weren't necessary. We were, needless to say, excited and ready to go to work.

The warehouse was only 1 of 2 that were oversized which was perfect for Score. Karen drew out the layout and design of the gym offices, seating area upstairs, kids play area, seating downstairs, color scheme, coaches offices and restrooms. Of course, the gym was going to be OU colors, red and white with black added in. We would later add on another half court as we grew so that we now had five basketball goals. Banners were put up, and signs outside and inside, and marking boards. In honor of Cary, we put up an "Excuse" banner and added a store later on.

The five goals were donated to us by a company named Jack Wills as a promotion for the Goalsetter basketball goals which are the best non-permanent goals you can buy.

When God gets ready to bless someone, He does so with purpose and perfect timing. Everything was falling into place. Business grew quickly. We worked really hard but God blessed our efforts. Karen and I decided to start looking for another coach. We had to let Craig go because he was lazy and acted depressed most of the time, which he had admitted to.

While shopping for a bed frame one night at Mathis Brothers in Tulsa, one of my former students and players on my AAU teams, Marcus Hall, took care of us as a salesman. That began a 10-year run of great fun and success with Marcus as my second coach.

One day, Karen was in the office working and started noticing that Marcus started sounding exactly like me; same words, voice deflections, phrases and sarcasm. We were a great team.

Meanwhile, the roller coaster of Aaron's life was spiraling out of control. He was arrested a couple of times for marijuana possession and was hanging around a tough crowd. One night, he called me and said that some really bad men were looking for him and he probably wouldn't survive the night. I went looking for him where he was staying downtown, but had no luck. My prayers were flooding through me as I was praying really hard. He survived the night but it was only a start to other difficult situations.

The phone call scared me to death, but I also knew and counted on God's promise to restore everything which included Aaron and I reminded God, Aaron was the most important person to be restored.

I remember thinking that surely I can't lose both my sons. What I wasn't counting on was Martha being restored. She also had gotten remarried and we had to work together on some things for Aaron, so she invited Karen and I over to her house.

Much to Martha's surprise, Karen went right up and gave her a big hug. They knew each other because of Cary. A couple of weeks later, Martha was at my gym so her and I could talk about Aaron and she confessed to me that she wasn't a very Godly person when she was married to me. I could tell a change in Martha but it would further show itself when we met at the tag agency to exchange some papers. Unfortunately, I didn't have what she needed and she got mad at me and accused me like before of always being selfish and self-centered. Later that day, when we had gotten things worked out, we met again. By God's grace, I told Martha that I was sorry for what I couldn't provide and that one thing I wanted her to know was how much I loved her and wanted the best for her. Martha apologized, which would have never happened before and told me she loved me also.

Over the years, we've met at a couple of places such as the court house for Aaron. He was now living with a young lady and they later had a child together named Danica which has given Martha and I even more time to visit as we attend Danica's functions at the same time. One day when I hugged her goodbye at the courthouse, she expressed to me that she never should have left. There was a peace and contentment I had never seen with Martha. It brought me great joy because out of a tragic situation of death and loss were left two broken people who God had now reconciled.

We were both remarried yet thankful to God for one another. Martha was always a nurse and gave great care to our son. Now she had a heart full of love and forgiveness to share with patients, co-workers and family. It may sound unusual, but I didn't want Satan to win any battles, especially over my family, even if it was my ex-wife. Karen and Martha like to tease me, calling themselves wife #1 and wife #2.

ADR in my Neck (only 1 this time)

CHAPTER 20

There is Always a New Crisis

"Nor height, nor depth, nor any
creature, shall be able to separate
us from the love of God, which is in
Christ Jesus our Lord."

Romans 8:39

"Nothing can wedge in between the love of God and the saint."

OSWALD CHAMBERS

(Baptist preacher and author)

Shortly after I got back from Germany, I started having nerve pain down my back and my left arm was going numb. About a year and a half before my surgery in December 2007, around June of 2006, I was riding my bike home from being at the park with Karen and my two step kids. My bike crashed into a large hole that was covered over by tall grass. Unfortunately, I flew over the top and landed on my head.

There really wasn't a doctor I trusted that well but as always, God would direct me. Karen and I were involved in building a youth all-purpose sports center with legendary basketball coach Eddie Sutton and his son Steve. Eddie's doctor that had performed back surgery on him was the well known Dr. Rogers.

I couldn't afford to go back to Germany because the last surgery had taken every dime we had saved.

Sure enough, my MRI showed a ruptured disc in my neck. A fusion was out of the question, but there were a couple places in the US performing a disc replacement as an experimental surgery. Dr. Rogers happened to be one of them. No one in the US was doing multiple discs and the US was using discs that were obsolete in Germany. My main concern was that the success of disc replacement depended on the number performed, (Karen's research). That's why we had to go to Germany instead of the US. Dr. Rogers was confident because I asked him point blank if he could do this. More importantly, my good friend, Dr. Phil Barton assured me that if Dr. Rogers said he could perform it successfully, that I could trust him because he was one of the best surgeons around. That was all I needed to hear. Through all of my back and neck problems, I had tried all kinds of treatments and many shots as well. As I said before, nothing ever worked or even helped, so here we go again.

Thankfully, the surgery went really well and within a few weeks, I was back to normal. My health kept getting better and my strength was returning. Doing sled work, playing pickup basketball games and riding on jet skis was becoming fun again. Remarkably, I was pain free for the first time in years. There were many blessings during this time. Karen wanted me to get another dog to replace the sadness of losing Franklin. I really missed him. She asked me to look at some border collies a couple hours away, thinking we were only going to take a look.

When I went over to the pen to look at the puppies, one in particular walked over to me and stood up for me to pick him up. He immediately put his head on my shoulder and I walked off with him. Karen told the owner that I guess we are going to buy a puppy.

We named him Boomer and he became my best friend. Soon after this, he started going to the gym with me. He was unlike any other dog because he literally played basketball. Boomer started playing defense on players and he would palm basketballs in his mouth and bring them to me. When I'd try to make a pass, he'd try to knock the pass down. He'd play catch with me and passed the ball well with his nose. Word got out about a dog who played basketball and a couple of TV stations and shows called to ask if they could do a story on him. Over the years, he gave great joy to many kids. It was fun watching him greet all the kids and players walking into the gym. He knew when to move out of the way and when it was okay to be in the action. There are so many pictures of him by my side at the gym. When he died of cancer, Karen and I cried for a week. We were so saddened by his loss. Only God could supply a dog to a basketball trainer who loved basketball. Every good and perfect gift is from above and Boomer was perfect.

"MY HEALTH KEPT GETTING BETTER AND MY STRENGTH WAS RETURNING. DOING SLED WORK, PLAYING PICKUP BASKETBALL GAMES AND RIDING ON JET SKIS WAS BECOMING FUN AGAIN."

After my back and neck surgery, which were about seven months apart, I had six years of great health. Everything was going well. Aaron was doing better and was working as a carpenter. He's really smart. One day he texted me, thanking me for teaching him to have a strong work ethic. He had been observing that a lot of the guys he was working with were lazy and didn't have any integrity.

A couple of months later, he sent me another text thanking me that I didn't let him watch all the garbage on TV. Now that he has his own daughter, he didn't want her watching all the stuff I had protected him from. I used to talk to him about things like movies, TV shows and books having redeeming value and he's mentioned the importance of that to me.

"Training Lee Mayberry of the Milwaukee Bucks."

Aaron has a love/hate relationship with me. Friends and family tell me that he blames me for everything, but he tells me he loves me and respects me and I believe him. He is still trying to sort out and understand God and everything that's taken place. He has been angry at God for so long and has taken his anger out on me a lot, but God has given me the grace to forgive him and accept him for where he's at. My prayer life has been strengthened over the years because of him.

One thing I finally learned was that there is always a new struggle or crisis and that contentment is a gift from God.

I lived for a long time hoping that the new crisis or problem would be handled soon and that something or someone's problems would be worked out and then I'd be okay or happy. Problem was, there's always a new crisis or a new problem.

I prayed that God would help me to live today and be content today. God has blessed me with the ability to live in peace and to not fear. He also taught me most importantly, to praise and worship Him in the midst of heartache and pain as well as to forgive others. I believe this is where my strength comes from. Being able to realize my battle was never against flesh and blood, but against powers and principalities helped me to forgive and to love others no matter how they treated me. I know that's God's grace. Being able to praise God even in divorce or great loss and not question God's faithfulness or love for me, had enabled me to not think of myself as a victim or someone who's mistreated or deserves better. My desire and focus has been to glorify God and thank him for all things perceived, good or bad.

My first basketball camp in Berlin, Germany. Great kids and coaches.

CHAPTER 21

Sharing Christ and Basketball in Germany

"Consider the lilies, how they grow:
they toil not, they spin not; and I say
unto you, that Soloman in all his
glory was not arrayed like
one of these."

Luke 12:27

"The things that make God so dear to us are not so much His
great big blessings as the tiny things, because they show us his
amazing intimacy with us."

OSWALD CHAMBERS

(Baptist preacher and author)

A friend of mine named Roscoe Magliore, was doing basketball training in a foreign country for Athletes in Action and I mentioned that I'd be interested in looking at something like that. He gave me the name of Mike Sigfried, who was responsible for helping AIA in foreign countries hook up with Christian coaches that would go and put on camps in these countries. It just so happened that Berlin, Germany was looking for such a coach.

AIA is a Christian organization with Campus Crusade for Christ who uses sports to introduce athletes to Jesus Christ.

Mike flew to Tulsa to meet with me and make sure I was the right person. The trip was set up for May of 2012. There were exhibition games set up for me to bring some players over to help in camp the first week and then train some club teams the second week. Four players traveled with me also, three of which I had trained that were now college players and another player that Coach Hoffman at Mercer University recommended to me.

"EACH YEAR, THE STAFF OR MYSELF WOULD PRAY WITH KIDS TO RECEIVE JESUS CHRIST AS THEIR LORD AND SAVIOR, OR TO JUST ANSWER THEIR QUESTIONS OF WHO JESUS IS AND WHAT HE CAN DO IN THEIR LIVES."

Each day, a different player or myself gave his testimony at the camp and then to the club teams we were training. We also trained a women's pro team that was fun. In the exhibition games, we picked up four players that were there to help in the camp. The nights we didn't play games, we'd take the players to Alba's practice gym and play pick up games. Alba is Berlin's professional team that had just built a new 15,000 seat stadium. The four players that spent the week with us have now become good friends. All four have traveled and stayed with Karen and I in Tulsa, Oklahoma.

They were a unique group that I've grown to love and care for. Lauranis now has a ministry in Lithuania and Taaved has a ministry in Latvia.

Frank does his own basketball program in Berlin and always helps with our camps in Berlin. Tobi is the assistant manager at the Nike store in Berlin, but is working on moving his family

"Speaking to the campers in Berlin."

to Tulsa because he loved it so much the month he stayed with Karen and I. By the way, I'm really nice to Tobi because he's a two-time national kickboxing champion in Germany. I've now returned to Berlin six times and every year, God puts the perfect group of coaches and players together. The camps are packed out and we help make it a great week of witnessing and training.

We always stay two weeks and do the camp the first week and train pro players or club teams the second week. The trip also includes a lot of sightseeing. Every year we rent bikes, or mopeds, and tour around Berlin. It's always my favorite thing to do. We also travel to Dresden or Potsdam, or Martin Luther's Church in Wittenberg, museums or any number of other places.

Each year, the staff or myself would pray with kids to receive Jesus Christ as their Lord and Savior, or to just answer their questions of who Jesus is and what He can do in their lives. The kids are from everywhere, Israel, Sweden, Russia, Poland to name a few. All of them become my favorites, because they are just kids like here in Tulsa. A couple of years ago, I was asked to give my testimony at a Church which was really hard because I talked about things I hadn't thought about for years or mentioned to anyone. This last year after I spoke, seven kids and parents came up afterwards and wanted to know more about Jesus. Every year is memorable such as visiting the concentration camp or seeing the castle that was never lived in. I'll never forget riding bikes the first year through Berlin with a group of players ranging from 6'3"to seven feet and getting a lot of stares. We were an interesting looking group riding bikes in a city of 3.5 million people.

As we were riding along, Kevin who was leading us yelled out to not look to the right into the woods, but everyone looked of course. It was a nude park and as Jeff Foxworthy would say, it was bad naked. It was a bunch of old guys best I could tell in the woods. Kevin tried to warn us.

Kevin Woods is one of the leaders of AIA in Berlin and has become a great friend as well as his wife Lisa, Leah, Tobi and others. I love catching up with everyone each year. My favorite experience is leading the coaches before camp each day in a 30 minute devotional and sharing what God is doing in my life and working to strengthen theirs. The part that I'm always amazed at is how God puts things together and how He always has a plan. The Bible promises that what Satan means for evil, God means for our good and His glory. I never would have done basketball training in Germany if I hadn't had surgery at Stenum Hospital and endured the pain of four ruptured discs. Oswald Chambers talks about being "broken bread and poured out wine" like Jesus for God's purposes. Like Joseph in the Bible, God receiving the glory in the end is worth the struggle and I've been blessed beyond measure.

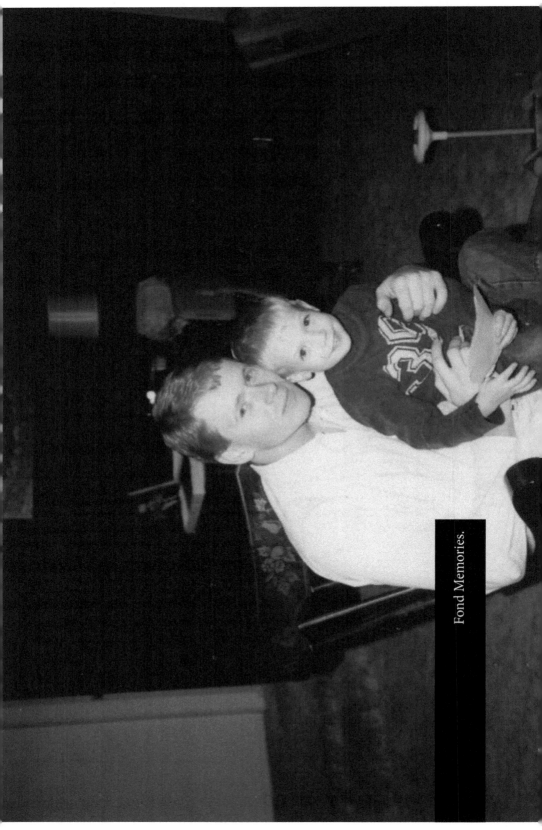

Fond Memories.

CHAPTER 22

In Pain, Trivial Things Become Unimportant

"But none of these things
move me."

Acts 20:24

*"As we go on in the Christian life it gets simpler, because we are
less inclined to say, "Now why did God allow this and that?"*
OSWALD CHAMBERS

(Baptist preacher and author)

The first year in Berlin of May 2012, I was shooting baskets while players were warming up. My left hamstring felt a twinge and I thought it was a stretching problem and I was needing to stretch out more. By the time I got home, something wasn't right. The nerve pain returned down my leg and my headaches came back.

The tests revealed stenosis of my spinal column. Structurally, I was sound and the ADRs and flexible fusion still looked good, but the pressure on my spinal chord and nerves were now causing the problems. The plan was for me to run the camp in Berlin, in May 2013, and then to travel to Bremen and Stenum Hospital to have another back surgery.

Karen needed to accompany me so that she could take care of me the two weeks in Bremen.

Karen was always great taking care of everything while I was in the hospital. It would have been too lonely and difficult without her. The encouragement she gave me during these times was very important. Often I've thought that God gave me the perfect wife as I would have never gone to Germany for surgery if not for her. Karen is fearless and confident and will do whatever it takes from building a gym in a warehouse, to heading for Bremen Germany to have strangers do an unknown surgery on me.

Again, we had saved just enough money for the surgery. This time, the hospital stay was a week and the hotel stay was a week. When I got back, I did the rehab myself. My back was structurally sound again, but would encounter struggles over the next six years.

God had a plan though as he always does. The problem after my surgery that was causing my pain now was scar tissue from all my injuries and surgeries. As always, we started doing research on alternative procedures, medicines and talking to everyone possible. There were hospitals and treatments in Switzerland, China and elsewhere that I looked into for answers. In the meantime, I tried all kinds of treatments and supplements and tinge units, none of which helped. After a couple years of intense pain, I heard from a friend about a procedure called Lysis of Adhesions.

There are a few doctors in the US that perform the procedure but Karen and I always go to the best so it was off to Lubbock, Texas to meet with Dr. Racz who is a world renowned pain doctor. As always, God provided as I was able to stay with Dr. Ranne who had moved his practice to a hospital there. He packed me up and took me to the three procedures and we were able to catch up on things.

The procedure was really cool to watch. There was a TV screen in front of me that showed the scar tissue breaking up as Dr. Racz was injecting the "cocktail" of medicines into my back. For 30 minutes, it was the most excruciating pain I'd ever felt. The two procedures the next couple of days didn't hurt nearly as bad but either way, I didn't care. Getting my life back was worth the pain for sure.

There were so many things I was missing doing; riding my bike and jet skis, playing basketball or just demonstrating during my lessons, playing tennis or just working around the house. Karen was great at helping me with everything but I missed being able to work hard. I've always been in good shape and it was depressing at times and a constant struggle to stay positive.

"KAREN IS FEARLESS AND CONFIDENT AND WILL DO WHATEVER IT TAKES FROM BUILDING A GYM IN A WAREHOUSE, TO HEADING FOR BREMEN GERMANY TO HAVE STRANGERS DO AN UNKNOWN SURGERY ON ME."

The procedure helped, but the scar tissue was extensive. Over the next couple years, I would need to have more procedures to remove the scar tissue.

Dr. Racz as I mentioned is a world renowned pain doctor (Google him). He told me that most back procedures are unnecessary and that most just need scar tissue removed. Dr. Racz is retired and left Lubbock, Texas. With God's help, I was able to track him down and talk with his coordinator who gave me his cell phone number. Dr. Racz agreed to continue to treat me which was critical because he continues to learn and develop the Lysis of Adhesions. He's a brilliant man and speaks all over the world. My wife believes the reason Dr. Racz wants to continue to help and cares for me is that I won't give up. Pain medicine isn't an option and I continue to work to get better. Dr. Racz has now invited Karen and I to stay at his house in the mountains of New Mexico.

Without Lysis of Adhesions as with the ADR's, I would be in intense pain and in a wheelchair. I had lost the use of my left leg before my first surgery and the doctors said I may or may not get it back. Gratefully, the nerves regenerated and I got both legs working for six years. Now, the nerve pain goes down both legs and causes nerve issues in both hips and my lower back. Staying ahead of the scar tissue is what we are working towards now.

One of the reasons I refuse to give into the pain is because the night before my last procedure, God had me read Psalm 41:3 and promised to restore my health. Over the years, God has graciously given me scripture from his Word to encourage me.

Each time, he is faithful to His promise. I'm confident this time, I can trust Him as well.

It's important to note that God never promised to heal Cary. He could have. My faith was strong enough and we prayed many times for him to be healed. I'll find out in Heaven the why's I believe, but until then, I don't question because I trust God that His plan is the best plan and that his love was demonstrated for me when his son Jesus Christ died for me and my sins. That's enough for me to trust him with my life. There's never been a difference to me between Jesus as my Savior and Jesus as my Lord. Because I trust him, he has the right to do with me as he chooses. As of now, I've had nine lower back and neck surgeries, procedures and numerous shots. As I'm typing this, I'm packing and headed for my tenth tomorrow morning. I used to tell Cary that he was killing my back with lifting his wheelchair and he'd just laugh at me. Of course, it was a labor of love and I wouldn't replace it for anything. There's no way for me to understand all of the reasons for my back issues, but trusting God is easy. If suffering for Jesus Christ and if going through struggles is necessary in God's plan, then I'm okay with it and thank God for every struggle and pain. One day when I face Jesus Christ, I want to hear well done my good and faithful servant. Everything will have been worth it then.

Pain and different struggles, for lack of a better word, has done a few things for me. First, it has kept me humble. I've known over the years, that I was totally dependent upon God as my source and supply. All of my abilities and successes are from Him. Being dependent on God I've learned, is a great place to be. His plans are always the best and I trust Him. When things looked the darkest, I knew God had a plan and that it was for my good and His glory.

Secondly, pain has kept me focused on what's important. God has always provided everything I need if I'd seek him first. In pain, trivial things become unimportant and being heavenly-minded is easier. My calling in life, to invest in children, has been my focus for all these years and it has been aided by physical and emotional pain and loss.

Third, my prayer life has been consistent and has grown because of pain. Not only do I know that I'm totally dependent upon God but I know that others are as well. The Bible says "the days are evil" and that everyday, every situation and word, thought and deed are important. When you're in pain, life has a seriousness about it, and I learned from Cary to make the most of each day. When I don't get to pray for my normal 1-2 hours each morning, for whatever reason, I'm missing the most critical conversation and relationship I can have that day. Prayer keeps me grounded, dependent, humble, and at peace. Pain has helped to keep me dependent on prayer.

Lastly, pain has caused me to have empathy for those who are hurting, physically or emotionally. My wife and I are starting a hobby farm for kids and parents who deal with handicaps, diseases or other difficult situations. We know how hard and exhausting life can be and want to be an encouragement and give families some relief and something to look forward to. Pain has helped take away self-centeredness and selfishness and keep my focus on others struggles. Pain will do one of two things:

It will cause a person to grow bitter, resentful, a victim mentality, negative and self centered; or like Cary, it will help a person grow in character, love and empathy. One allows pain to have a redeeming value and the other a life of emptiness and self-centeredness.

Don't get me wrong, at times the pain was unbearable. Like after Cary died and I didn't want to live anymore because there was nothing in life I wanted to continue. I drove my corvette one night going 150 mph, wishing I could end my life. I wasn't going to, but I wanted the pain to be over. I was tired of being numb and not feeling love or hope in life and I didn't see an end in sight. Then I'd go home, get back in the Word of God, and let Him remind me of Jeremiah 29:11 and the hope and a future that He promised me.

My sister Deana, who's known as much pain and loss as myself, wrote this letter to me just recently. Writing this book has brought back a lot of tears and tough memories, but her letter helped ease the pain and once more put things in perspective. She wrote me:

> "When I think of Cary, I think of how much he liked to tease. Relentless. I thought he was just the cutest child I had ever seen with that blonde hair and little grin that was always on his face. He was happy and kind and thoughtful, meaning he thought of you and asked about you. No child does that but Cary did. I remember those hands. I remember him with Ben, (his cousin) and the video games and I tried so hard so he'd be happy. The best part was when Franklin (his service dog) came into our lives and he belonged to Cary. That was a huge gift to him and I loved that bond between them. I could just sit for hours and enjoy those two. Cary was stubborn but I understood it. You put

Cary and Aaron together and I was not a big enough person to babysit them by myself! Wow, but I appreciated the love and relationship/ bond between them. Talk about ornery though. I really think the two of them together, took it to another level! I keep pictures of me and Cary and me and Aaron on my cedar chest in the living room to remind me. They just have a special place in my heart. Cary really liked to discuss things. He used to frustrate me with comments he'd make that he believed the Bible said and I'd argue and say no that's not right but every time he'd see me, he'd say it again. I was not going to change his mind. Funny thing is now I know he's right. Just took me longer to see it. He was so particular towards the end where we'd go eat and what he'd eat and what he'd do and it was good to let him boss us around and be in control of the situation because I can't imagine what that was like for him. But boy was he sure of what he wanted. I remember all the difficulties and how unthoughtful people treated him. We all did the best we could with what we knew but I wish I had it all to do over again. I'd hope I'd be more mature and better at it now. That we'd know how to talk to, how to love and support and see the needs and make all of your lives better. To bring joy and happiness and to know how to do things better. To say the things I should have said.

I would give anything to hear him say "Dad" one more time the way he used to. It was the sweetest thing to my ears. The way he loved his Dad was just something special. The rest of us just had to take a back seat to that relationship, as it should have been. I just will never forget all of his questions. He was always thinking. He liked to see me squirm, to gross me out, to shock me, to boss me, to tease me. We loved memorabilia stores and animals he could hold or touch. He did not like to be treated like a baby and I never wanted to make him feel that way. I looked through photo albums and those were the happiest times of my life. You just knew how Cary felt about you and I truly looked forward to getting to spend time with him every single time. He gave me a purpose and my life perspective.

I don't like to think about all the pain and struggles so I can always come back to his laugh, his orneriness (meant in a good way though) his "How are you doing Deana?", his faith in God, his love. To me, it all added up to one wonderful and extraordinary human being I got to have for a nephew. I didn't enjoy him taking off in his wheelchair but I did understand it. Couldn't blame him. - Love Deana"

Myself, with one of my students, Ryan Lofton, who also went to Uganda with me. One of the 10,000 kids I have trained over the years

CHAPTER 23

Even a Coach Needs a Coach

"In everything give thanks: for this
is the will of God in Christ Jesus
concerning you."

1 Thessalonians 5:18

*"The circumstances of a saint's life are ordained of God. In the life
of a saint there is no such thing as chance."*

OSWALD CHAMBERS

(Baptist preacher and author)

Being confident in my abilities as a basketball trainer was
no problem, but being confident in my business intelligence
was another thing. Working hard wasn't the issue, but I knew
there was so much about business I didn't understand or
know. It was never an issue of success. Scorebball.com had
been in business for 16 years and we were always packed out.
Marcus started with me in 2008 and we stayed busy six days
a week ever since.

However, I knew there had to be a better way of doing
business. Karen was now working for me and we were doing
everything ourselves. For 12 years, I had worked alone. So as I
always do, I began to pray that God would give me someone
that could help me run a smarter, more effective business.

We didn't need help with the basketball part, but with the business part. First thing I did was hire a tax service and turned everything over to them which took care of a lot of busy work. I hate paperwork anyway. Next, I had become good friends with Coach Eddie Sutton's son, Steve and was training his son. Out of the clear blue, as I hadn't mentioned my prayer to him, he suggested I call a guy named Clay Clark who was the former U.S. SBA Entrepreneur of the year, a successful business owner and coach. (see Thrivetime show) God provided the perfect person. I began to meet with Clay once a week and we looked at every detail and changed everything. He would give me homework to accomplish every week from how we did billing, to how we hired, to marketing and everything else you can think of.

> **"ALL WHO OBEDIENTLY ENDURE UNTIL THE LORD ACTS ON THEIR BEHALF ABIDE IN HIS FAVOR."**

One of the most important things I did was hire someone to do the office work (i.e. an office manager) and free Karen up to do work she was gifted at and enjoyed a lot more. Later on, we hired a full-time receptionist. We started scaling everything and creating checklists for everyone to follow. Our advertisement budget increased, but became more turn key and productive. Since we started all the changes, business has steadily increased and just about all the jobs have been delegated to someone on the staff.

We tried hiring another coach for a few years, but as Clay reminds me, you have to go through a few (about 10) knuckleheads to find a winner. It's become apparent that hiring character first is what matters. There's no way to be successful if you don't. After 9 years, Marcus and Kelly, his wife, started fostering kids and finally decided to adopt 3 kids which I'm very proud of. He reluctantly decided to take another job so he'd be home in the evenings and on Saturdays. As always though, God would provide a former college player that most importantly, loves God and wants to glorify Him with his life and work. All who obediently endure until the Lord acts on their behalf abide in His favor. We can expect to be blessed if we wait upon the Lord. Each time we needed something, a gym, coach, or receptionist, God has provided.

On the walls of our gym are banners that were put up to influence kids and parents thinking because the Bible says "as a man thinketh, so is he." One banner has a list of excuses such as too short, too slow, tough life, and many more, that I put up in honor of Cary. As I mentioned before, there's never been a tougher, more stubborn person. Yet, there also hasn't been a more righteous, caring and loving young man. He never used excuses.

On another banner is a list of character qualities that we work to instill into kids. If ever there was a person who had a reason to feel sorry for himself or to be bitter and question God, it was Cary, but that wasn't him. He was a young man of character. He was instead, my inspiration to do the right thing no matter how much pain or disappointment I endure.

My wife and I have tremendous goals for our future planned. I've always wanted to play the guitar, so I recently started lessons. My wife and I got our scuba diving license and we have trips planned to dive some beautiful oceans. She also for my birthday, got us a skydiving excursion and we survived.

We are now in the process of building our farm which will include our hobby farm for kids going through difficult times. Karen is also planning on doing horse shows and competition for her English riding and jumping.

There are still "struggles." My back and hips still hurt most of the time. I'm scheduled to have both hips replaced as I now have severe arthritis in both joints. My dad has Parkinsons and my mom just recently had heart surgery. Aaron, my son, is still struggling in life and hasn't returned to the Lord Jesus and my sister's husband is still in prison. There will always be struggles and that's okay because, as is my habit, I refuse to fear and worry or complain. Instead, I will take everything to Him in prayer and trust God for my present and future. He is faithful and can always be trusted. Just recently, God started talking to me about doing something new. (Isaiah 43) He even confirmed it by speaking to my mom late at night when she couldn't sleep. She didn't understand what she was telling me, but I did.

After 25 years, I'm stepping aside and taking a non-coaching role at Score Basketball. As always though, God provided the perfect person to take over, my assistant Courtney.

In some ways, it's very sad because Score has been my "Oasis" through many storms and trials.

There was always a place to call home that I knew would bring me great joy and satisfaction, even when times have been so difficult. It's hard thinking of giving it up, but God is my leader and one to be followed always.

I don't know what God is going to lead me to next, but I know it will be something perfect. It will be where I'm supposed to be according to His plans for me and that is always good with me. When God does something, he always does it much greater than we thought possible.

2 Chronicles 20 will attest to that and is one of my favorite stories of the Bible. This battle is not mine, it's the Lords.

Throughout the Bible, God gives the same instructions for whatever we are going through, and that is to rejoice in all things, pray about everything, and to give thanks in all things. These habits have carried me through a life of great blessing and favor. They will carry you as well.

Afterwords

I didn't want to write this book. God had to send me so many messages to convince me that I needed and was supposed to write it. From numerous friends telling me I needed to, movies and stories that God would use, to so many passages in the Bible where the Holy Spirit would have to convince me that I wasn't just imagining things. "Me? Write a book?!" was my reaction. I was embarrassed to tell anyone I was writing a book. My wife figured it out after awhile. There was a lot of arguing with God and procrastination that He disciplined me for a few times. He had to get my attention and He certainly did.

First, my new truck was damaged in two places, then I had chest pain where I checked into the hospital and then my horse bit me on my back. That hurt and I think God probably laughed at me over that one. I spent two hours in traffic in Dallas just sitting there, waiting on construction to clear. Shortly after that, I spent three hours trying to get my phone fixed and couldn't get it working right. Finally, after about the tenth "message sent," I decided I better listen. The book then became a priority and I gave it the attention He wanted me to. Surely God, no one wants to read a book about a boring person who has led an unimpressive life. I'm about as average as you can get.

Then God reminded me that I'm exactly the person that He calls to do the extraordinary because I am ordinary.

He took a slow, short, white kid and sent him to OU to play on a great team and then eventually to start a basketball program that would one day train around 10,000 kids, from all over the US to Germany and Latvia and Lithuania, and Poland. Who am I to doubt God could use a book from someone like me when he used all the average characters in the Bible and did miraculous things with them and through them; Moses comes to mind. I did pray that God would do something spectacular and not average if Cary had to die. It's just like God to surprise me beyond what I can imagine. It was hard writing about painful memories and reliving old wounds.

It's November of 2020 and I've just had 4 more surgeries this year. That makes 14 in 12 years.

First, I had one of my hips replaced and then a couple of months later, the other one. Not only did my pain go away in my hips but my back pain is gone also. For the first time in years I'm without pain and Karen says I don't walk funny anymore.

Next, I had eye surgery to replace a lens and a few weeks later the other one was done. My vision is much better and I can even read a menu now. Like my friend Courtney said to me: "It's like God was giving you a year off to further fulfill His promise to restore you."

I don't know if God speaks to others like He does me. I don't know why he'd give me all those promises and glimpses into the future. The guess is, I needed it. I'm no one special though and I've never thought so.

I do talk like He's my dad though and my friend and so He is. My closest of friends who happens to be the God of the universe. He loves me desperately and wants to spend time with me. He promises me that he will save every tear I shed and that one day very soon I'll get to see Cary and he and I will spend an eternity together enjoying each other, in His presence. I look forward to worshiping Jesus in person some day and tell Him face to face how much I love Him and appreciate Him dying on the cross for mine and Cary's sins so that we could be forgiven. I don't want to ever take that for granted.

CPSIA information can be obtained
at www.ICGtesting.com
Printed in the USA
BVHW022141160621
609642BV00013B/2507

9 781736 421727